Discover

Your Blind Spots

HOW TO STOP REPEATING EVERYDAY BUSINESS MISTAKES

Dr. Bob Smith

Discover Your Blind Spots

How to Stop Repeating Everyday Business Mistakes

Client Edition

Dr. Bob Smith

Clear **Direction** inc.

Discover Your Blind Spots: How to Stop Repeating Everyday Business Mistakes

Dr. Bob Smith
© 2004 by Robert Kinsel Smith
All rights reserved. Published 2004.
Printed in the United States of America.

Clear Direction, Inc.

4314 Newton Court
Dallas, Texas 75219
(214) 520-0520
www.cleardirection.com

ISBN 0-9755921-090000

Library of Congress Cataloguing-in-Publication Data has been applied for.

Jacket design: Steve Connatser
Editor: Dan Barrett, Esq.
Copyeditor: Ray L. Young
Interior design and composition: Ray L. Young

For all who ever ...

- do something they later regret,

- need people to do what they say they'll do,

- need to get another person's attention,

- want to be better at hiring and promoting others,

- want to do a better job than most in business,

... this book is for you!

Contents

Thank You

As with all things in my life, this book is possible only because of the help of many friends. Everything that I have, I have received from others, and this book is no different.

First and foremost, I thank my wife, Jill, who loves me, supports me, and stirs me toward excellence in all things.

Second, I express appreciation to Dan Barrett, who rewrote and edited the entire book, reshaped the format, clarified concepts, and added characterizations for easier understanding; to Ray Young, who copyedited and formatted the entire book; and to Greg Link, my agent and counselor on every aspect of marketing, formation, and distribution of this book.

Next, thanks and gratitude to those who have read different manuscripts, helped with the naming and formatting, and given overall and specific comments that have shaped the book into its present form. These include Tish Visinsky, my associate; Dr. Virginia Harvey, chairman of the Department of Educational Psychology, University of Massachusetts, Boston; Pamela McCann, president of the McCann Group; Will Marré, former president of Stephen Covey and Associates and now CEO of ReaLeadership; Bob Pike, CEO of The Bob Pike Group; Fred Harburg, Chief Information Officer, Fidelity Investments; Gunnar Selin, senior partner, Profiles4Professionals; Gerry Smith, CEO, Saxon Publishers; Dr. Zenglo Chen, industrial psychologist, Motorola Corporation; Chuck Stewart and Nick Gaede, partners, Bradley, Arant, Rose & White; Claude Ramer, Assistant General Counsel, IdleAire Technologies Corporation; Brian Derksen, Senior Officer, Deloitte & Touche; Bob Dedman,

Chairman, and Doug Howe, EVP, ClubCorp; and Rich Meiss, of Meiss Education.

The reshaping and forging of the concepts in this book happened in the fires of the everyday working worlds of some of my clients; to them, I am grateful. This forging happened from interaction and discussions with these clients as they challenged and applied the concepts to their businesses. These clients include executives at Motorola; Fidelity Investments; Pro4Pro; The Archon Group; Crescent Real Estate Equities; Saxon Publishers; Energy Spectrum Capital; Hinckley, Allen & Snyder law firm; Haynes and Boone law firm; Powell, Goldstein, Frazer and Murphy law firm; Brown McCarroll law firm; The Petrous Group; and all of my colleagues at the Robert S. Hartman Institute for the Advancement of Formal Axiology.

Gratefully,

Dr. Bob Smith

Preface

Our brains betray us. My brain betrays me. Your brain betrays you. We rely on our brains, believing that they supply accurate, dependable conclusions. And fortunately for most of us, those conclusions are accurate enough for us to be able to function with a modicum of success.

But our brains don't let us know when they are limited in their perspectives, nor do they warn us about those subjects that send them sideways. We all have blind spots, and we don't know those until it's too late! All of us have subjects about which and situations in which our brains don't see what's really going on. It is in these times that we trust something that is not trustworthy. We think we understand, when, in fact, we don't; and this is why, when we act on these thoughts, we, as well as others, needlessly suffer the consequences.

We carry on through our days, believing that we can function effectively, unaware that our own thinking biases skew our perceptions. We also expect others and ourselves to be able to function at full strength while we ignore the effects that different conditions have on our brains. We blindly trust our brains—when they are actually blindly leading us astray.

I wrote this book for people who want to be more effective in their relationships and who are not satisfied with the same old ways of doing things—when those ways don't work very well. While the principles apply to all aspects of life, the examples and applications in this book are derived from my work and research in business.

One of my professional activities is to help people better know and use their strengths in business contexts. Since 1987, I have used the Hartman-Kinsel Profile to help my clients increase their understanding of how their own individual thinking biases result in strengths and blind spots. The good news is that our own thinking biases are fairly consistent, so awareness and helpful adjustments are not moving targets. This makes it easy for us to learn about how we think, see how and when our own blind spots make us vulnerable, and then do things that reduce the negative effects of our thinking biases.

Over the years, I've noticed that when people have disagreed with the results of their Profile reports, most often their colleagues would confirm that the Profile descriptions were accurate. I have also noticed that all my clients have had employees who acted differently depending on who was present and that "problem" employees would never act improperly when I was around. These observations drove me to investigate what was happening—what processes and forces were at work.

My research revealed a phenomenon that I have called the "Thinking Condition Effect" or "TC Effect." Simply put, the TC Effect is *the phenomenon that under different conditions we think (and therefore act) differently.* I have also observed that ignoring the TC Effect is one of the principal causes for many recurring problems. When people ignore the TC Effect, they—

1. repeat mistakes that are avoidable,

2. endorse theories that just don't work, and

3. develop inaccurate views of themselves that lead to continual personal and professional problems.

Ignoring the TC Effect makes you naïve about yourself, people, communications, agreements, and hiring and promoting employees. It also causes you to trust what is untrustworthy and to repeatedly utilize strategies and implement policies that don't work.

A salient example of this is the common practice of interviewing candidates for jobs. Industrial psychologists know that no statistically significant correlation exists between how a person performs in an interview and whether that person will be successful in that job. Yet many business people still select a new employee based on their feelings about the different candidates from the interviews! My research proves there are people who are "gifted" interviewees—the ones who always get the job offers when those offers are based on interviews. The problem is that these candidates, who interview so well, often do not perform in the jobs nearly as well as the candidates who interview poorly. The TC Effect blinds interviewers to what they are looking for. Knowing about the TC Effect challenges normal interviewing practices so you will be able to make better selections.

This book introduces the TC Effect and then applies it to five key management tasks. Recognizing and understanding the TC Effect enables people to more accurately know and use their strengths, employ sound business practices, and abandon the practices that, while common, are ineffective and counterproductive.

My Guarantee

Learning about germs and using that knowledge to develop appropriate hygiene practices enables us to reduce the spread of disease. In the same way, the awareness you gain from this book and the practical suggestions interspersed throughout it will allow you to develop new levels of awareness and effectiveness. In all likelihood, you already know most of the things contained in this book. But in the reading, you will appreciate more fully and understand more clearly what you already know. That comprehension will *compel* you to do things differently.

I guarantee that if you learn how the TC Effect affects you and others, and you make simple adjustments based on this new awareness, you will be significantly more effective at work and at home.

—Dr. Bob Smith

Author's Note

English does not have a singular pronoun that functions for both sexes. Using "s/he" or "her/his" is cumbersome, at best. For ease of reading and not as a reflection of gender bias, I use masculine pronouns throughout this book. If you find this usage offensive, please accept my apologies in advance. I made this choice when I was in Condition II thinking; please accept it as such.

Part One

Why Our
Abilities Vary

Different Conditions Affect Our Ability to Think

Larry tossed the sales reports onto his desk in disgust. Jackson's expense reimbursement requests exceeded budget by 20 percent for the fifth month in a row. Hadn't Larry and Mark, Jackson's supervisor, discussed this problem—not once, but twice? Mark had assured him that he would talk to Jackson about the problem and that it would be fixed. Why couldn't Mark simply lay out the rules for his people and make them toe the line? Did Mark's brain go blind when he was away from Larry?

Jonathan shook his head in disbelief as the fourth department manager in a year left his office, on his way to Human Resources to collect his severance. All the people Jonathan had hired to fill the position were qualified. They all looked good on paper and impressed him during their interviews. Once they actually settled into the chair behind the desk, though, none of them had been able to handle the demands of the job.

What was he doing wrong? Why couldn't Jonathan find someone who lived up to the potential they showed during the interview process? Was Jonathan actually blind to certain things when he was interviewing candidates?

Bill closed the door to Don's office carefully. Don (the CEO and Bill's boss) had left the shareholders' meeting furious and had just finished yelling at Bill because production was still not up to the needed levels. Bill knew that if he slammed the door, Don would fire him on the spot!

Yes, production was down again. But why couldn't Don understand that working the kinks out of the new logistics system took time? If they could just stay on course for another couple of months, the numbers would improve. Don did not need to be jumping on Bill's case in the middle of the project. Was Don blind to what it really took to turn things around?

D o the preceding situations or the following questions have a familiar ring to them?

- Did you ever wonder why sometimes people perform like stars during an interview and flail like a gasping fish when it comes time to do the job?

- Have you ever left a meeting, confident that the others in the group knew what they were to do, only to have them act completely differently than what you discussed?

- Has an employee given you feedback that indicates he hasn't understood a single word you said during his review?

- Have you noticed that people seem to have good judgment and insight at certain times and seem to be blind in their thinking at other times?

Performance Depends on Conditioning and Conditions

"I can't believe it!" Tom seethed disappointment, frustration, and anger.

"I ran as fast as I could! Look at that time—it's pathetic! I'm not getting better—I'm getting worse! I just can't try any harder. I'll never make the state meet at this rate. This isn't worth it—I quit!"

During graduate school, I had coached distance track and cross country at a local high school. Every year, I knew I would get this kind of reaction from at least some of the students, and I would prepare for it. It was important that each runner have a great experience and perform to his potential. How they trained and when they ran their toughest races made all the difference in how they performed at the end of the season.

7

Chapter 1:
Different
Conditions
Affect Our
Ability to
Think

Ours was one of the best high school track teams in the country. The team was full of gifted, experienced, and dedicated runners who were focused and who pursued their goals passionately. For most, running was fun; but reaching their goals was also serious business.

As their coach, I had to individualize practices in light of each runner's goals, taking into account each person's experience and conditioning needs. A big part of my job was to make sure their confidence grew along with their strength, endurance, and experience. Every season tested my abilities as a coach.

When runners had been sick or injured, it wasn't too difficult to encourage them to hang in there. They expected their performances to suffer under those circumstances. The greater challenge for me was during mid-season when the younger, less-experienced runners performed below their expectations for reasons they couldn't understand.

During the middle of the season, strength training inevitably took its toll on young muscles, and performances lagged behind what they had been at the beginning of the spring. No matter what I said or did, younger runners always got discouraged as their race times crept upward. They couldn't seem to understand that their fatigue was a natural effect of the conditioning and a necessary stage to their end-of-the-season goals.

They assumed that as long as they continued to work hard, their improvement would be constant—that each week their times would drop until they reached their goals at the end of the season. Talking to them before their races and pointing out what was reasonable for them to expect and what was likely to happen didn't seem to help. After their races, after they tried their hardest and did their best, they fought back tears when they didn't accomplish what they hoped and wanted to accomplish. They didn't realize that *success requires proper conditioning as well as proper conditions.*

In Athletics as in Life

"I thought you said Gene is a great tennis player," Joey said.

"I did and he is," I replied.

"Well, because you said so, I invited him to play as my doubles partner in the club championship last weekend. He was terrible! The other team figured out pretty quickly that he was good for an unforced error anytime they hit the ball to him. We got killed in the first round!"

"You doofus. You knew he has been out sick for nearly a month. He just came back to work last Wednesday. Of course he played horribly—he was in lousy condition!"

The truth is, Gene is both a good and a poor tennis player. He is quite good when he is in good physical condition and on his game. He is easy to beat when he is sick, weak, and out of practice.

9

Chapter 1:
Different
Conditions
Affect Our
Ability to
Think

In life, as in athletics, the circumstances under which a person performs are as important to the outcome as the condition the person is in at the time of performance. When we ignore one or the other element of the equation, we often are unpleasantly surprised by the results.

A runner's physical condition affects his speed and agility. Altitude and humidity affect his ability to use oxygen. Our physical, emotional, and mental conditions *and* the circumstances we find ourselves in affect our ability to think and make good decisions.

You can't accurately assess a person's ability to perform without considering both the condition he is in and the conditions he is under.

Internal and External Conditions Affect the Way We Think

These days, I coach executives and professionals instead of runners. I still face many of the same situations I faced with the kids at my school. I find that I must continually look beyond the obvious and focus on the effects of conditions to understand why people think, decide, and act the ways they do.

In coaching business professionals, I integrate the latest advances in technology and formal axiology (the science of thinking) to determine how various internal and external conditions affect our ability to think. Recent advances in and research using formal axiology have enabled me to confirm and describe, with precision, the effects of conditions on our thinking.

I have observed that behaviors change as circumstances change. And I have observed that behaviors change *because* circumstances change. The conditions within which we think and make choices affect how well and how thoroughly we think. This phenomenon is what I call the "Thinking Condition Effect," or the *TC Effect*, for short.

We think differently when we are discussing things over a cup of coffee with friends than when we are under a deadline to act and our career is on the line. Although we are the same people, housed in the same bodies, with the same histories, values, and desires, we in fact use different parts of our brains in those two different contexts. Our priorities and abilities to consider different alternatives and exercise judgment truly change, depending on the circumstances.

We use different parts of our brains, in varying intensities, depending on how much fear, pressure, or stress we feel at the time. The part of our brains we use and the conditions under which we use them determine our perspectives and choices.

As We Think, So Do We Act

Few would disagree that Greg Norman, recently inducted into the PGA's Hall of Fame, is a great golfer. He is in the top twenty in career earnings. He has won almost too many professional tournaments to count, including the British Open, twice. But he is a perfect example of how the condition one is *in* and the conditions one is *under* can drastically affect one's ability to perform.

In 1986, Norman blew a four-shot final-round lead in the PGA and shot a final-round 78 to lose the U.S. Open after leading going into the last day. In 1990, after being tied for the lead for two days, he shot a 76 to fall nine strokes behind the co-leader and fell out of contention at the British Open. In 1996, he squandered a six-shot lead on the last day of the Masters to lose by five strokes.

11

Chapter 1:
Different
Conditions
Affect Our
Ability to
Think

Greg Norman's varying performances under the extreme conditions of PGA Major tournament play illustrate what is true for everyone: the conditions in which we find ourselves—the shape we are in and the circumstances we are under—affect the way we function.

This book will help you understand the four general conditions that affect your thinking. These conditions are true for all of us and affect us in similar ways. As you read this, you will better understand how the different conditions affect how you think, make decisions, and take actions. These categories are broad so they will be easy to remember and use.

When people understand and take into account the effects of conditions on their thinking, they are consistently less frustrated with themselves and others, and their overall effectiveness increases dramatically.

The conditions in which we find ourselves—the shape we are in and the circumstances we are under—affect the way we function.

What About You?

Are you open to discuss difficult topics, willing to take the opinions of others into account, or are you close-minded and dogmatic?

In conversations, are you kind and respectful of others, or are you curt and dismissive?

Do you plan carefully and thoroughly, or are you impulsive, jumping right into action once you have a vague idea of the goal?

Are you patient and calm, trusting that everything will come in its own time, or anxious and hasty, needing things to be done yesterday?

If you are truthful—or if we ask your colleagues to answer for you—the answer to these questions is likely "yes" to all of the above characteristics, at different times, depending on the situations.

When the conditions you find yourself *in* and the conditions you find yourself *under* vary, your actual capabilities of responding to the situation change. While you may be patient and calm or kind and respectful as a rule, in certain situations it is not likely that you will be anything other than impulsive or self-centered.

This is true of everyone. The good news is—you can do something about it! Once you understand how conditions are affecting you and those with whom you come in contact,

- communication will be more effective,

- decisions will be more productive,

- goals will be easier to achieve, and

- life, in general, will be a lot better.

The first step in this procedure is to understand how you think—why thinking blind spots exist, what happens when data goes into your brain, and what determines your decisions and the actions that result.

13

Chapter 1:
Different
Conditions
Affect Our
Ability to
Think

14

*Discover Your
Blind Spots:
How to Stop
Repeating
Everyday
Business
Mistakes*

Chapter 2

Your Brain—
A Committee of Six

Before I begin discussing the Four Conditions—the parameters within which virtually all thinking takes place—I need to review a little about the process of thinking itself.

We process information and reach conclusions—make decisions—using our brains. With the 1990s being the "Decade of the Brain," exactly how the brain works has become one of the most studied and investigated subjects. Entire courses of college and post-graduate study are devoted to such questions as "What is consciousness?" and "How do we arrive at meaning?"

Researchers have proven that the brain does not function as a single bundle of nerves acting as a single processor.[1] The various parts of our brains and how those parts function independently can be likened to the various parts of our bodies and how those parts function independently. When we walk, we coordinate many independent parts of our bodies, including our muscles, nerves, vision, and inner ear, to move forward smoothly, avoid obstacles, and maintain balance. When we think, we coordinate different independent modules, or clusters of neurons, to reach a conclusion or make a decision.[2]

As you read the next few pages, you will see that just as we have physical strengths and weaknesses—or preferences—such as being right-handed or left-handed, our brains also have unique strengths and weaknesses that come from preferences. Certain modules are dominant and therefore play a major role in how we see and understand things. Others are "quiet," not participating to the same degree. And it is the interplay of these six thinking modules—the way they interact, their varying strengths, and the ease of use—that leads to our personalities, strengths, and weaknesses.

A Committee of Six Modules

Picture a committee of several different individuals, each operating independently and having specific duties, acting together to set policy for an organization. Each person on the committee constitutes a "module" with a certain perspective or responsibility. When all of the modules are working as they were designed—when each is properly doing its job—perspectives are not ignored or mishandled, decisions are made, and actions are taken.

We know that our brains work like a committee, even though researchers are only beginning to understand exactly how the brain works and are not even in agreement about the best ways to study it.[3] Different modules of the brain process different things, by coordinating different neurons for the task. Each module is responsible and suited for specific kinds of processing. When all of the different modules of our brains do what they were designed to do, our decision-making is efficient and coordinated. When a certain module does not do its job, we do not get the benefits that would normally come from that module.[4] We misinterpret or misunderstand the situation because we process the data with another module or group of modules that are poorly suited for that job.

The following description of thinking will not be a review of the work of neurophysiologists or molecular biologists, because brain studies are still very rudimentary. These scientists have made great advances over the past decade in understanding and mapping how the different parts of the brain work, but they have a lot of discovering to do before they are able to accurately describe the functioning of the different parts of the brain, let alone the entire brain.

Formal axiology, the science of thinking, helps us by defining the six ways that make up how we understand and know things. Breaking our thinking into six functional parts is a simple but useful way to study our brains' outputs. The following description is a functional explanation of the nature of thinking.

To begin, I conclude that a different module of the brain handles each of the six categories of thinking. Our brains are, therefore, a great "thinking committee," comprising six key "modules," each of which has a specific job to do in processing information.

Three of these six thinking modules determine how we understand the world; another three, how we understand ourselves. You will see that I have titled each module according to its output or what that module is thinking about, not according to its location in the brain.

The three modules you use to think about the world:

♡ the Intuition and Empathy module

◯ the Practical module

▢ the Structured module

*Discover Your
Blind Spots:
How to Stop
Repeating
Everyday
Business
Mistakes*

The three modules you use to think about yourself:

♡ the Inner Self module

◯ the Outer Self module

▢ the Self-Concept module

Just as we differ in our physical characteristics, we also differ in how we use our different thinking modules. And just as people can be distinguished from one another by how they walk, so too, our individual personalities can be distinguished by how and in what proportions we use our thinking modules.

People who tend to use the Intuition and Empathy module when thinking about people are concerned with others' feelings, what they care about, and how they will respond. People who prefer to use their Structured thinking modules will focus on how others measure up to specific standards or whether they fulfill the letter of the law, whatever it might be. Our different personalities are the result of our using our six different thinking modules in different ways from how others use theirs. These differences lead to the combinations of our preferences, feelings, choices, and actions that form our unique personalities.

Thinking Committee Members

When we say we *know* something, we mean that we have used our different thinking modules to assimilate and process data and information. Three modules give us three different ways that we can know or evaluate people and things outside of ourselves, while the other three modules give us three distinct ways to know or evaluate ourselves. Each of these modules processes in a particular way and brings its own perspective to the thinking "meetings" of the thinking committee.

This idea of different "ways of knowing" has been the focus of philosophers for centuries. While philosophers knew the three categories of knowing for centuries, it was not until the mid 1950s that Dr. Robert Hartman precisely defined their properties and integrated those with a formal mathematical system. Having such a system enables formal axiologists to model thinking, just as physicists model the physical motion of things with mathematics. But rather than introduce Dr. Hartman's work[5] here, I think a better way to illustrate the different ways we know things is from a conversation I had recently with a group of executives.

Early one day, I had been visiting a close friend, David, who has a measure of fame in the industry common to a group of men with whom I was visiting. I had worked with David, and over the course of many years we had shared family celebrations, supported one another through family members' illnesses, and developed a close, personal friendship.

One of the younger executives in the group brought up a recent newspaper article about a project David was spearheading. He said, "I don't know him, but I've heard a lot of good things about him and certainly know about the successes he's had with his company. Do any of you know him?"

Another member of the group nodded his head. "Yeah, I know David. We served on an ethics committee together."

At that, the senior executive barked, "Sure, everyone knows David. You stand in the same room with the guy and you 'know' him. You read about him in the papers and you 'know' him. Give me a break—you don't know him. All you did was attend some meetings he chaired. You may have even played in a golf tournament with him. But you don't know him, just as I don't know the Pope!"

That conversation demonstrated the three ways we can know other people:

1. **Personally**—We have a relationship with them on a personal level; we have shared heart-touching life experiences; we know and care about their inner concerns and personal feelings. Philosophers call this *intrinsic* value— understanding that the intrinsic nature of something is the singular nature that is true to that unique object or person. They call it "value" because "to value" is "to know."

2. **Publicly**—We have done things with them professionally, know them in the practical roles they play, know how they compare with others, or have had social interaction with them. This kind of knowing is called *extrinsic*, relative, or practical value.

3. **Academically**—We know things about them as a result of information received from sources such as the media, a résumé, or something someone else has said—something other than personal contact. This kind of knowing is based on data, facts, or ideas and is called *systemic* value.

Three Modules for Thinking About the World Outside Ourselves

The *Intuition and Empathy* module processes people and things in personal ways (things of the heart). *Do you know Sally? Yes, we have been friends for 16 years; we were in each others' weddings, attended one another's kids' baptisms, and have been through good and tough times together. I love Sally.*

The *Practical* module processes people and things from a relative, practical, and casual standpoint (the circle: things that are practical—like the sun or a wheel). *Do you know Bill? Yeah, he's a great accountant. We worked on the Data General project—we really did good work on that one! I like working with Bill.*

The *Structured* module processes people and things against expected standards and definitions in a black-and-white analysis (things that fit in the box or within standards). *Do you know Bill? I know he graduated from UCLA, got an MBA, joined the firm in 1995, and is licensed as a certified financial planner. I know things about Bill.*

Three Modules for Thinking About Ourselves

22

*Discover Your
Blind Spots:
How to Stop
Repeating
Everyday
Business
Mistakes*

The *Inner Self* module processes our inner feelings and senses of our individual unique value and identity—who we sense we are. *I am comfortable with who I am, so I am not knocked out of commission when someone rejects me.*

The Outer Self module processes our own practical and public identity—how we appear, our likes and dislikes, and how we fit and function in the world. *I am good at what I do, am able to contribute effectively to the team, and am very aware of how my actions and how I appear lead to how others view me.*

The Self-Concept module analyzes how we measure up to our standards for ourselves—whether we embody our ideals and meet our expectations for ourselves. *I should not quit, because I gave my word. It is my responsibility; therefore, I should do it. I know I am a good planner, and I have a personal goal that I should be able to retire by the time I am 62.*

Six Modules Making Up One Thinking Committee

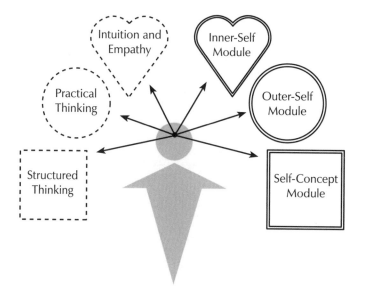

In the early days, brain scientists believed that each bump of the brain was a node that did one specific task and was not involved in other tasks. Research has proven this view to be inaccurate.

While scientists do not yet know exactly how the brain works or all the ways the different areas of the brain interact, they do know that the brain is immensely complex, that the different parts of the brain work together to do specific tasks, and that some parts even do multiple tasks.

The idea of thinking modules is accurate when you picture that a module is not a specific, small part of the brain but is a number of different clusters in the brain (recent research indicates that some "thinking" is done outside the brain, as well) that are usually close to each other, working together to do a specific task.[6]

Natural Thinking Structures— Module Use in Everyday Life

All of us have our own unique ways of using our thinking modules—ways that lead to "thinking biases" and "thinking blind spots" that are peculiar to us alone. Our use of our modules in our own ways forms the foundation supporting how we view virtually all phenomena. Our biases are the result of both nature and nurture—we were born with certain biases (nature), and we developed other biases in response to our environments and life experiences (nurture).[7]

An important thing to remember about your biases is that they are often invisible to you (thus the term "blind spots") and that you hold them firmly. Most of them don't change easily. They create the framework or "structure" for the thinking you do all the time.

Your thinking structure directs how you think and therefore is the source of your own personality. Your structure is the foundation for your natural thinking strengths and can trip you up—causing you to misinterpret and respond inappropriately to situations in which you find yourself. What are you biased toward on a regular basis? What do you see but regularly ignore because your blind spots take over? Which thinking modules do you depend on and which ones do you ignore?

Consider a person who is consistently very empathic and has poor practical judgment—notice how the two characteristics align with two of the world thinking modules. This person will be sympathetic, caring, and trusting *to a fault*—because he is using the empathy part of his brain all the time, while, on the other hand, he is unaware of the political dynamics happening in social or work groups and has no awareness of the practical consequences of different actions because he does not use the practical thinking module in his brain enough.

This personality type would arise (simplistically, since I am talking about only two of the six modules) from a thinking method that "requires" him to search for the inner, intrinsic goodness in people while it causes him to be blind to what they actually do. His thinking bias would lead him to cultivate the kernels of inner goodness, even though this over-belief often grows weeds and chokes the garden. A human resources director with this thinking structure would be blinded from seeing the value of comparing applicants against one another. He would prefer to hire a candidate whom he has gotten to know personally, because "he is a good person" or "has potential." He would prefer to not compare this candidate against others because "that would discredit the candidate's unique value as a person by treating him as a commodity that can be compared to others."

How the Modules Interact

Success usually requires cooperation—coordinating many thinking modules

Just as walking requires coordinating many different parts of our body, most situations call for using more than one thinking module. A manager reviewing a moderately successful employee's performance must balance his imposing strict expectations (structured thinking) with the importance of his giving support and encouragement (intuition and empathy). The effective managers are those who know how to and are able to coordinate their thinking modules and not rely on just one or a few thinking modules.

An Aside:
Regarding "Personality Conflicts"

When you understand that personalities are the result of how we think, only then are you able to see that there really is no such thing as a personality conflict. Managers regularly fall into the trap of defining conflicts between people as "personality conflicts."

Conflicts arise as a result of people valuing (thinking about) the same things in different ways. A common "personality conflict" occurs when one person is rude concerning a colleague's abilities or performance. The conflict is really caused by one person's attacking a colleague's abilities or contributions based on how he *values*. The two people are valuing the same thing differently. Actually, their personalities have nothing to do with the conflict but, like the conflict, are the results of how differently the two people value or think.

This distinction is critical—because defining a conflict as a personality conflict leads to the conclusion that no suitable solution exists. "Well, that's just the way they are—we have a personality conflict on our hands, and there's really nothing anyone can do about one of those!" Lasting solutions require accurate diagnoses of the causes of the problems. Defining the situation as a personality conflict will always lead to futile attempts at restoration.

When we understand that the conflict lies in the deeper roots of how the people are thinking, evaluating, and valuing, then we are able to define the conflict, address it, and find clear direction to a lasting resolution.

This need for coordination is reviewed extensively in Chapter 11.

Each thinking module has its own priorities and ignores the concerns of the other modules

Your eyes don't hear sound. Your fingertips don't process visual images. Each thinking module in your brain likewise does what it was designed to do without concerning itself with the responsibilities of the others. As a matter of fact, there is even a specific part of your brain that is responsible for putting together the different perspectives—but it is always subject to the input it receives from the different modules.[8]

Just as any committee has some members that are more assertive than others, your individual thinking committee is not in perfect balance. Some of the modules are stronger than others. Sometimes, the resulting imbalance leads to people using the wrong thinking modules to finalize their conclusions.

For instance, couples who start mom-and-pop stores often ignore the practical and analytical aspects of business ownership. They focus instead on fulfilling a lifelong dream. They ignore market research, planning, and due diligence because these factors don't fit within the framework of their thought processes. It is no wonder that 90% of all businesses fail within the first year of opening their doors.

Each thinking module has its own characteristics that cannot be understood from the perspective of the other modules

Just as our different senses handle different properties that have no meaning to the other senses, our thinking modules handle different things that make no sense to the other modules.

People in business often refrain from acting or making a decision for fear of making an error. This fear can be so strong that they ignore their own track records of success, the support they have from others, and the fact that they are the only ones in the position to make the decisions.

From a logical, analytical perspective, this fear does not make sense. The module that processes logic has no patience and sees no validity in fear. "If it makes sense, then do it; if it doesn't, then don't." Each module has its own perspective that doesn't make sense to the other modules.

Everyone has thinking biases—preferring to use some modules over others

Most people favor one hand over the other. While most soccer players naturally have one leg that is stronger than the other, effective players develop the ability to use either foot with equal precision; otherwise, they will be too easy to defend. Our brains function like our bodies in this regard. We all have thinking modules that we prefer to use and other modules that we would rather not use; but to be effective—to not fall prey to brain blindness—we must be able to use all six modules and to do so when most appropriate.

The experience of using the "weaker" thinking modules is often just like the experience of using a weaker or less-developed part of our bodies. When a right-handed person has to write with his left hand, he immediately feels frustration and wishes to write with his more-developed right hand. When we have to use a thinking module that is less developed, we prefer to revert back to thinking with the modules that are easier for us to use.

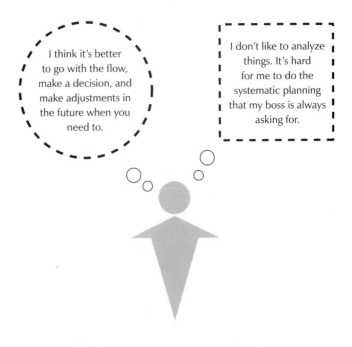

When we use a thinking module that is not well suited for the circumstances at hand, we will misunderstand the situation or the consequences

Our different senses are suited for certain tasks and are unable to help with other tasks. Our eyes cannot process smells and our hands cannot effectively process light waves. This is true with our thinking modules, as well. Each handles specific properties and, when called on to deal with other things, leads us to misunderstanding and inaccurate conclusions.

For example, many artists personally connect (empathize) with their works and are unwilling to think about them with their Practical thinking modules. This unwillingness blinds them when they need to sell their art because they don't use the practical-thinking part of their brains to handle the practical situation. Using one thinking module to process a situation when another is better equipped to do so results in misinterpretations and inappropriate choices.

Most people use a different thinking method when thinking about other people than when thinking about themselves

Commonly, we are clearer and more accurate in our thinking about what is best for our colleagues or friends than about what is best for ourselves. This is why it is easier for most people to develop and carry out strategic plans for business activities than to design and put into practice a meaningful and clear strategy for their own lives.

"I don't know why people don't do what I suggest they do; it's just so obvious to me when they are making choices that limit their successes," says the manager who never applies the counsel he gets from others.

Since they come from different perspectives, our thinking modules sometimes reach opposing conclusions

To your eyes, a skunk is a beautiful animal. But your nose tells you it's disgusting. Likewise, your thinking modules function independently and can end up with conflicting conclusions. It is common to have a feeling—intuitive thinking—that you can't trust a certain person, while the objective facts—structured thinking—indicate that you should trust that person.

People differ from one another. I often speak with business managers who have learned over the years to trust their intuition, even when the logical part of their brain argues against doing so. But I also talk with managers who have learned to never trust their intuition but rather have learned that their particular strengths lie in analysis and logic.

When our thinking centers disagree, it is imperative that we know which ones are usually accurate and under what conditions they work best.

34

*Discover Your
Blind Spots:
How to Stop
Repeating
Everyday
Business
Mistakes*

Each of us has adapted so that our thinking committees aren't simply an unruly cacophony, incapable of concerted action. In the end, the preferences or biases we have form our thinking structure—the foundation upon which we make decisions. It is comforting to realize that these structures exist for everyone and that no one's thinking is perfectly balanced among all six modules.

This thinking structure constitutes the condition a person is *in*. Our environment—the world and the circumstances in which we find ourselves—provides the conditions we are *under*.

It Is *You* Doing the Thinking

How you use your thinking modules is how *you* think. If you write holding the pen in your left hand, *you* are a person who writes left-handed. You can choose to write holding the pen in your right hand, but you probably won't if that causes you pain or frustration.

If you prefer to use only five specific thinking modules and don't use the sixth, then it is *you* doing that kind of thinking. If you decide you are going to include the sixth module in your decision process, then, again, it is *you* doing the thinking. While your biology and biography result in certain biases and preferences about which thinking modules you prefer to use, you'll see that the two deliberate thinking conditions described in this book enable you to use more of your brain than you tend to use on a regular basis. So any discussions about parts of your brain doing certain things is really about *your* thinking. This is not a description of something being done to you—it is what *you* are doing.

The Four Thinking Conditions

Chapters 2 through 5 will examine the four thinking conditions—the contexts in which we use our thinking modules. Consider the following contexts:

- Trying to get an employee to explain a complex procedure when he feels intimidated by others in the meeting.

- Having a person agree in a meeting to do something that he has never done before and then being surprised when he doesn't do it.

- Interviewing a candidate and finding that he acts totally differently once he is on the job.

- Using a "universal" management technique you learned from a book and later experiencing low morale or turnover problems in your team.

- Giving feedback to your best employee and learning that he thinks he is a failure.

- Believing you can discuss a complex subject with someone who has just come out of a stressful and exhausting meeting.

These situations illustrate a disconnect, a state of affairs in which the participants are not only *in* different conditions but also *under* different conditions. For ease of use, I have titled these conditions with descriptive names: *Relating*, *Reflecting*, *Responding*, and *Reacting*.

Various things characterize these four conditions. One of the key points, however, is how many members of the thinking committee get a voice in the meeting—which modules are working or are able to work. This difference among the four conditions constitutes the TC Effect, for these thinking conditions affect how we use and don't use the different parts of our brains—when we see and when we are blind.

The first condition, Relating, is the most positive and productive—and is the one in which all of the thinking modules are likely to be activated—yet it is often underutilized. It is the condition I have been more careful to use than any other in writing this book. We'll see why in the next chapter.

Discover Your
Blind Spots:
How to Stop
Repeating
Everyday
Business
Mistakes

Notes

1. "The brain is a highly modular organ, with each module organized around a particular computational task." (Gregory Hickok, Ursula Bellugi, and Edward S. Klima, "Sign Language in the Brain," *Scientific American*, June 2001, p. 65.)

2. "So just as specific members of a large orchestra perform together in a precise fashion to produce a symphony, a group of localized brain areas performing elementary operations work together to exhibit an observable human behavior." (Raichle, "Visualizing the Mind," *Scientific American*, April 1994.)

3. *Summary*: Some brain researchers believe the best way to organize a study of the brain is by regions, while others believe the best way is by functions. Regional investigation directs the neurophysiologist to focus on one particular location and determine how it works and what it does. Functional studies direct the neurophysiologists to study the outcome of the brain's functioning and then to determine which parts of the brain were working to get that result and what roles each of the different participating parts played.

   Marsel Mesulam, "From Sensation to Cognition," *Brain*, Oxford University Press, Vol. 121, 1998, pp. 1,013-1,052.

   John Medina, *The Genetic Inferno* (Cambridge, UK: Cambridge University Press, 2000).

4. "The root of anxiety disorder may not be the threat that triggers it but a breakdown in the mechanism that keeps the anxiety response from careering [*sic*] out of control. . . ."

   Summary: It is believed that stress anxiety can be caused by an overactive amygdala (too much fear awareness) or by an underactive pre-frontal cortex (not enough "Everything is OK").

   Christine Gorman, "The Science of Anxiety," *Time Magazine*, June 10, 2002, pp. 46-54.

5. A thorough presentation of the history and foundations of formal axiology can be found in *The Structure of Value* by Dr. R. S. Hartman (Southern Illinois University Press, Champaign, Illinois, 1967).

   Dr. Mark Moore has posited a more comprehensive theory of the nature of thought by integrating quantum physics with formal axiology. His conclusion is that the physical nature of the different ways we know things and ourselves is consistent with the properties of the different waves in quantum mechanics. Dr. Moore concludes that the physical nature of our thoughts, the interaction of atomic particles, is the same as the nature of the thoughts themselves.

Mark A. Moore, "A Quantum Wave Model of Value Theory," *Formal Axiology and Its Critics* (Atlanta: Editions Rodopi, 1995), edited by Rem Edwards.

6. Raichle, "Visualizing the Mind," *Scientific American*, April 1994.

Michael S. Gazzaniga, "The Split Brain Revisited," *Scientific American*, July 1998.

Tyler, Russell, Fadili, and Moss (Cambridge University), "The Neural Representation of Nouns and Verbs: PET Studies," *Brain*, Vol. 124, No. 8, Oxford University Press, 2001, pp. 1,619-1,634.

John Medina, *The Genetic Inferno* (Cambridge, UK: Cambridge University Press, 2000).

7. "For some time, we have known that development results from the dynamic interplay of nature and nurture. From birth on, we grow and learn because our biology is programmed to do so and because our social and physical environment provides stimulation."

Sara Gable and Melissa Hunting, "Nature, Nurture and Early Brain Development," *Human Environmental Sciences*, University of Missouri, Missouri, pub. GH6115, August 1, 2001.

John Medina, *The Genetic Inferno* (Cambridge, UK: Cambridge University Press, 2000).

8. Raichle, "Visualizing the Mind," *Scientific American*, April 1994.

Part Two

The "Thinking Condition" Effect— Sometimes 20–20, Sometimes Blind

Chapter 3

Condition I—Relating

"I can't believe we came up with that answer! None of us working alone could have done it, that's for sure. Man, we were cooking! But my brain hurts from all the contortions it has been through today. I'm glad we got together to attack this thing instead of everyone trying to go it alone."

D esign teams know, comedy writers know, trial attorneys know. You know.

Maximum results come when you get a group of people together in a setting where they can focus, where they won't be interrupted, and where they are free to interact—bounce things off of each other without having to worry about anything but the problem at hand. Professionals are so convinced of the benefits of this kind of process that they sometimes invest a great deal of time and money to arrange the process, hiring facilitators and the like.

This is Condition I thinking: *Relating*.

Condition I thinking is extreme thinking—cognition in overdrive. Participants relating in a Condition I session are free to interact with focus, without being defensive or needing to advance any other agenda. Ideally, there are no deadlines. Everyone is not only entitled to be included but also necessary to the process. Different perspectives are encouraged and considered. Everyone is responsive to and respectful of everyone else.

When we are relating (Condition I), we are able to use all of our brain—every module can be engaged because we are being stimulated and energized by the other participants. Thus the biases that would normally result from our individual thinking structures are reduced or eliminated. We push one another to think more fully, giving and receiving energy to think and stay on the subject. We introduce new or unfamiliar perspectives to one another, forcing us to use parts of our brains that we normally prefer to avoid. Every member of our own thinking committee gets to have its say in the deliberations.

44

*Discover Your
Blind Spots:
How to Stop
Repeating
Everyday
Business
Mistakes*

*— when we relate, we interact and see
things from others' perspectives too —*

Forms of Condition I Thinking

Condition I thinking occurs in a variety of daily settings. When a manager strategizes with someone who reports directly to him about the best way to secure a new account, win a contract, or fix a problem, the two are relating and are in Condition I. The input they receive from each other is forcing them to think in ways and consider perspectives they normally ignore. The energy and differing perspectives of the other person kick dormant thinking modules into gear. The brain fires on all cylinders.

Meeting with another person is not always a Condition I situation. Condition I requires that the context be free from stress among the people, with everyone feeling safe, included, and valuable—and focused on the task at hand rather than on their own needs.

When an employee discusses with his human resources director how to handle a problem with a colleague, they are usually in Condition I. They bounce ideas off of one another, considering multiple viewpoints, factors, and outcomes. They actually spend more time and expend more energy thinking about the various factors than they would if they pondered the situation alone or apart from one another.

While this activity may not be as robust or complex as a large group of people doing strategic planning for a business, this form of relating in Condition I thinking engages and stretches the participants so they use more of their brains in more ways than they do when contemplating alone.

Characteristics of Condition I Thinking

Condition I is called *Relating* because our thinking is stimulated, energized, directed, and encouraged by communication with other people. Their perspectives force us to think in a broader, more comprehensive way. The energy we receive—and are required to give—compels us to think more deeply, longer, and more deliberately than we would on our own.

Everyone's brain has the same six modules. Different people prefer to use those modules in different proportions—the members of your thinking committee are the same as mine, although the dominant members of my committee are likely to be different from the dominant members of your committee. In fact, chances are that one of my timid members will correspond with one of your bossy ones.

The input and energy we receive from other people in Condition I emboldens the quieter members of our thinking committee so that the more domineering members are forced to yield the floor, at least long enough for everyone to have a say in the process.

Points to Remember About Condition I Thinking

The way we use our thinking modules, and the number of our thinking modules we use, is the distinguishing characteristic of the four thinking conditions. In Condition I thinking,

- We use more of our brains than in any other Condition.

- We get the benefit of others' perspectives.

- We get the benefit and encouragement of others' energy.

- We are forced to look at things in ways we ordinarily would ignore.

For example, a Condition I invitation might sound like this: *"Why don't we have lunch and discuss it? I'll bet if we put our heads together we can come up with a solution."*

Condition I—Relating	
Gain thinking energy from others?	Yes
Benefit of others' perspectives?	Yes
Time and energy to think?	A lot
Effects of personal bias on decisions	Low
Average portion of all thinking modules used	100%
Decision errors and/or regrettable actions	Few

Condition I is the first of two conditions that are *deliberate* processes—processes in which thoughtful consideration, energy, and time are given to consider various perspectives.

Condition II—the other deliberate condition that involves this kind of conscious calculation, is what we will examine in the next chapter.

The Four Thinking Conditions

Deliberate Thinking	Automatic Thinking		
• Energy assigned to thinking before acting or deciding • Time taken to consider different perspectives • Gain the benefits of others' input and perspectives			
Condition I	**Condition II**	**Condition III**	**Condition IV**
Relating	?	?	?
• Low stress • Enriched conclusions • Energy from others			

48

*Discover Your
Blind Spots:
How to Stop
Repeating
Everyday
Business
Mistakes*

Chapter 4

Condition II—Reflecting

"I need to spend some time planning what I'm going to say. Let me have an hour by myself to study and get my thoughts together."

"Now, what was it our management trainer said I should do? I know there was something I was supposed to watch for when reviewing Jane's performance. Maybe I'd better take a look at my team directory and re-read my notes. Oh, yes! Now I remember. I never would have thought of that angle, but considering the trainer's rationale, I believe it will be a very valuable first step in this review."

Why do you take notes in a training class? Obviously, so you can refer to them later. They have value because the instructor gave you information you didn't have or a perspective different from your own (or both) that you can use as tools when you find yourself in situations to which they apply.

During a performance review, you mark what your manager tells you because it is something that will help you be more successful. Again, obviously, you couldn't come up with it on your own (or didn't realize it was desired behavior) or you would have already implemented it.

We read books, attend seminars, and listen to tapes to benefit from the experience of others. We broaden our perspectives and obtain understanding that can help us when we are contemplating issues in our lives.

This is Condition II thinking: *Reflecting*.

Condition II is a state of reflection, time spent considering different choices while alone, yet calling on the wisdom and experience—but not the direct energy of—others. Our thoughts are conscious and deliberate. We make an effort to consider different viewpoints and alternatives. We devote considerable energy to the task of thinking.

In Condition II, most (but not necessarily all) of our thinking modules are involved in the decision-making process. Since we are not engaged in an immediate, personal interaction with someone else, though, we may still tend to ignore the shyest or least assertive members of our thinking committee.

Learning from books is usually a Condition II event. We *reflect* on the author's input, which gives us a fresh point of view while we bring our own energy and commit time to the thinking task.

Forms of Condition II Thinking

Condition II thinking is quite common. Good managers typically are thoughtful and deliberate in preparing performance reviews. They examine personnel files for pertinent information. They may even think back on reviews they themselves have received and consider which techniques encouraged and which techniques had the opposite effect.

Supervisors find themselves in Condition II when they are contemplating how to handle poor morale on their teams. Books on management and conflict resolution sell like umbrellas during a sudden storm because supervisors know that the authors can provide solutions they couldn't find on their own.

Attorneys engage in Condition II thinking when researching legal questions. They will read not only court decisions but also law-review articles or white papers to learn from others faced with similar situations, hoping to borrow from those experiences to develop effective strategies for dealing with their clients' pressing problems.

Auto mechanics find themselves in Condition II when the way to fix a car's problem is not immediately apparent. Usually, they will put their tools down and pick up a manual that describes the various systems of the car and the ways they interrelate. They may refer to troubleshooting guides that give suggestions of things to check for specific problems. The best mechanics know that the input and experience of others can be very helpful in getting them to recognize something that has eluded them.

The likelihood is very high that you are in Condition II thinking—Reflecting—right now, as you read this book. Hopefully, you are gaining some additional perspectives you normally don't consider and are thinking about things with a greater deliberateness and attention.

Characteristics of Condition II Thinking

Condition II is called *Reflecting* because it is done when we are alone, in a contemplative state, weighing alternatives and considering perspectives often stimulated by outside sources. It differs from Condition I in that we are not interacting with a live person, so we are not receiving energy from others. Nor are we getting their feedback or active interaction on the ideas or opinions as we are forming our own.

In Condition II, we are using more of our brain than we normally would, since we are considering perspectives and opinions in addition to our own. We are nonetheless limited because we are filtering these viewpoints through our own biased thinking structures and are willing to consider new perspectives only as long as we have energy to do so. While our biases will still tend to keep our quieter thinking modules subdued, the outside input and perspectives do cause us to think with more breadth than we normally would.

Points to Remember about Condition II Thinking

In Condition II thinking,

- We devote time and energy to the thinking task.

- We consider different perspectives and information from sources outside of ourselves.

- As a result of this outside influence, we are using more of our thinking modules than we normally would.

- Since we are thinking by ourselves, we are vulnerable to our own biases and filters and thus are likely to not be using all of our thinking modules.

Condition II—Reflecting	
Gain thinking energy from others?	No
Benefit of others' perspectives?	Yes
Time and energy to think?	A lot
Effects of personal bias on decisions	Moderate
Average portion of all thinking modules used	67-83%
Decision errors and/or regrettable actions	Few

Conditions I and II are those in which we do our best thinking. We put most of our brains to work on the problem at hand. We don't rush to action. We consider the options and the consequences. The decisions we make as a result of Condition I or Condition II thought are usually good ones. We usually will have no cause for regret.

Therefore, it is often wise to:

- set aside time to read materials written by people who are successful in their respective fields,

- set aside time to reflect on your work and responsibilities apart from the frenzy and demands of each day, and

- initiate meetings with others to interact and Relate about matters that are significant to your effectiveness.

Relating and Reflecting

One of the most successful CEOs in American businesses in the 90s would hold unusual meetings with his board of directors. While most boards spend a lot of time addressing the financial aspects of the business, this CEO believed that the best way his board could serve him was to interact with him about important matters. Each board meeting would begin with a very short discussion of the financials of the business, because all of the board members had been able to review (reflect on) the financial information before the meeting. Then the CEO would say, "Here's what I am facing . . . How would you handle this situation?" Almost always, the topics were strategic in nature, and the board would spend the next hours relating with each other about how they would deal with what the company was facing. That CEO believes that those reflecting and relating sessions were the key to his company's success.

Unfortunately for most people, the two deliberate thinking conditions, Conditions I and II, account for a small percentage of their thinking activity. While these are the ones that normally deliver the soundest conclusions, they are the ones that are least common in most work environments and in our personal relationships.

54

*Discover Your
Blind Spots:
How to Stop
Repeating
Everyday
Business
Mistakes*

The next Condition is the one in which we spend the vast majority of our time. But it puts us into a condition where our blind spots begin to be problematic, similar to having to choose a family pet while blindfolded or without a sense of smell. It limits how much of our brains we use and therefore causes us to be vulnerable to errors in judgment.

A Condition II request: "Could you set aside fifteen minutes by tomorrow to review what I've written and write your comments on this piece?"

In Chapter 5, we'll take a close look at Condition III and learn to recognize when we should rely on it and when we should not.

The Four Thinking Conditions

Deliberate Thinking		Automatic Thinking	
• Energy assigned to thinking before acting or deciding • Time taken to consider different perspectives • Gain the benefits of others' input and perspectives			
Condition I	**Condition II**	**Condition III**	**Condition IV**
Relating	*Reflecting*	?	?
• Low stress	• Low stress • Richer conclusions because of the input of others from materials and memories.		

56

*Discover Your
Blind Spots:
How to Stop
Repeating
Everyday
Business
Mistakes*

Chapter 5

Condition III— Responding

"I heard what you said. I'm not interested. I never buy things I haven't re-searched myself, and I'm not going to start now."

"Don't talk to me about what other companies are doing or what other managers let their employees do. We have never had a daycare facility here, and we're not going into the kiddie-sitting business now. That settles it. I really need to get back to my work, and so do you."

We make decisions by reflex all day long, responding to various stimuli without seeking outside guidance and with little deliberate consideration of the alternatives.

First thing in the morning, an employee asks for a day off. The manager of a different department needs help with a minor crisis. A person under our supervision asks for direction in completing a task. Our stomach rumbles and we decide where to go for lunch. While no method exists that can accurately measure how much of each day we use responsive, automatic thinking, *it is safe to conclude that this Condition is the most common of the four.*

This is Condition III thinking: *Responding.*

Condition III thinking looks like a reflex—a simple, knee-jerk response to the situation at hand. It requires little energy. While some evaluation takes place, we consider only those perspectives and options that are part of our ordinary mindset. Our thinking committee is on autopilot, not even considering whether all of the appropriate thinking modules are engaged. And only those modules that we are comfortable using are engaged. The strong ones rule the process, while the weaker ones remain silent.

For those who know us well, our responses are predictable. We follow familiar patterns of reasoning, functioning as though we had been conditioned to function a certain way. We don't give much attention to either the subject matter or the process. Our personalities and how other people assess us are the result of this kind of thinking and the actions that come out of it.

—something happens and we respond—it's how we go through our days—

Forms of Condition III Thinking

A manager receives a request for a capital expenditure and responds with a question, "Is the item included in the budget?" He doesn't take the time to review his notes from management class or undertake a benefit analysis—his reflex response to a monetary request is to inquire if it's budgeted. No fuss, no muss.

An employee wants to work four ten-hour days per week, rather than the company's standard five eight-hour days. His supervisor immediately says, "No, that's not our policy." The supervisor doesn't take the time to consider the request and determine whether it might actually increase the employee's morale and productivity. He simply responds by reflex, from long-established practice. No energy is expended in the decision—he just decides.

A plumber makes a service call to a house because the bathtub won't drain. He uses a plunger. When that doesn't work, he goes outside and opens the clean-out valve. Water pours out, so he goes to his truck, gets his line auger, snakes it into the sewer line, and begins the process of clearing the clog. He had no need to consult a manual or get another opinion. The situation fit within well-recognized parameters, and he responded as he always does to the same circumstances.

Old jokes about doctors responding to virtually any complaint with "take two aspirin and call me in the morning" illustrate Condition III thinking. No purposeful analysis of the symptoms takes place. The doctor simply notes that a complaint is made and then responds by rote, prescribing without studying whether the remedy is suited to the malady.

Condition III thinking does not require a lot of effort or energy and is the thinking condition people use most often.

Condition III Strengths

It's not all bad news! Automatic, reflexive thinking has significant value. It is predictable. That can be a very good thing. People who are consistently effective in assigned roles usually are so because of their Condition III thinking patterns.

If the thinking-committee modules that you prefer to use are particularly suited to the situations in which you most often find yourself, your Condition III decisions will be suited to the situation. This condition is common for people who are fortunate to have natural strengths and biases that are consistent with the requirements of their roles.

For example, some salespeople have a seemingly uncanny ability to read people because their natural intuitive thinking is so clear. Successful politicians usually are gifted with naturally clear practical thinking. In these cases, using their natural strengths works for them; and their Condition III thinking, while not being perfectly balanced, is well suited for their tasks and leads to conclusions they can rely on.

It is important to know your Condition III thinking strengths. Business managers suffer needlessly when they have a sense of their strengths without an appropriate confidence that those strengths are trustworthy. When a particular aspect of your Condition III thinking is strong, we think of it as a natural strength, one that requires little energy and that consistently leads to desired outcomes.

Learn When Condition III Is Appropriate

Over the years, I've spoken with hundreds of business people who have expressed doubts about whether they could trust their hunches. They would get gut feelings and then find themselves analyzing and second-guessing those impressions. Sometimes, their scrutiny would lead them to abandon their gut feelings because they couldn't logically justify or defend them. Sometimes this self-doubt is a mistake.

When a person has very clear intuitive Condition III think-ing, his hunches will usually be very accurate. For these people, concerning these kinds of matters, Condition III thinking is more accurate than Condition I or Condition II thinking! The intuition is so sound that discussion of or deliberation about their hunches often leads to confusion or inappropriate questioning of the intuitive senses. Many successful business people have learned to "trust their gut," even when they cannot explain or defend their feelings to their colleagues when in Condition I sessions.

Most people have natural thinking biases that result in particular strengths. That is why it is so important for a person to know his natural strengths—so he does not second-guess himself when doing so would be harmful.

Our natural thinking biases—the structures or frameworks discussed in Chapter 1—lead to our strengths in Condition III settings. On the other hand, those same biases breed Condition III weaknesses—blind spots—as well! That's why being familiar with your Condition III thinking biases and abilities is crucial—it is important to know when you can rely on your own perspectives and when those perspectives betray you.

Rationalizing—Recognizing Condition III Weaknesses at Work

When Condition III responsive thinking leads to problems or causes us to be ineffective, we tend to rationalize our Condition III thinking process. In other words, we develop life philosophies that support our biased perspectives of our natural Condition III thinking.

Why? Because Condition III thinking is the easiest—it does not require thinking energy. We get to use our energy for action, which seems to be easier than using it for thinking.

Condition III is the method of thinking most of us use to function on a day-to-day basis. It is the mode we are in while riding the elevator, answering the phone, and talking in the halls. It's familiar and it's easy. Responding is like flying on autopilot and requires little or no investment of time or energy. It fits like a pair of well-worn jeans.

Which is not to say we're lazy. But it's a fact that, all other things being equal, humans will usually opt for ease and familiarity over struggle and distress. In fact, our preference for the security of the habitual sometimes makes us expend considerable energy protecting it. Our domineering thinking modules are jealous of their leading roles. They can make us come up with all kinds of "reasons" for keeping the other modules suppressed, actually supporting the negative effects of our blind spots, even if doing so results in repeated problems, pain, or loss.

Here are some common rationalizations one hears (or might use) to defend not investing the time and energy to consider others' viewpoints or perspectives:

- "He hasn't been through what I've been through."

- "He just doesn't understand my situation."

- "What he thinks about our department is based on inaccurate information."

- "He hasn't been successful enough to have a valid opinion."

- "It's against company policy."

- "He isn't as smart or insightful as I am."

- "He's just too young and inexperienced to understand."

- "He's too old and out of touch to know what's going on."

- "My mind is made up! End of discussion!"

- "This is who I am. I can't have any other view."

Business trainers can be good examples of people rationalizing their Condition III thinking biases. Most trainers are in Condition III while lecturing or leading classes. They are more or less following a script, not really taking the time or expending the energy to consider other alternatives because their energy is assigned to doing their task, not to considering new alternatives.

The trainer decides what the rules of the classroom will be, how they will be enforced, on whom he will call for what task, what material he wishes to cover, and what material to ignore. If someone protests about the relevancy of the material or the timing of an assignment, the trainer is prone to disregard the comments on the basis that those employees are less informed, lazy, or immature.

Alter the Circumstances

My research has shown that each person's thinking biases are very consistent and usually remain that way unless addressed. But my research (as well as the research of countless others) also has shown that we can change how we think about things and how we think about ourselves. (The Center for Brain Health in Dallas, a leading medical facility for brain injuries and Alzheimer's, has done extensive research and therapy over the years debunking many previously held views about the permanence of certain functions of the brain and proving that people can change how they think and how they use their brains.)

Sometimes, awareness and a simple adjustment will cure the problems produced by thinking biases and blind spots in Condition III. The following true story is an example of responsive Condition III thinking causing a problem that was easily remedied once the person was made aware of the problem:

"When we first started in business, my partner came in one day and told me that people didn't like to talk to me on the phone. They said that I always sounded annoyed, as if they were interrupting me.

"I was aghast. I certainly didn't want to give them that impression.

"When I thought about it, though, I realized that people who called on the phone were, in fact, interrupting me and that my automatic responses conveyed that to them.

"I moved my telephone away from my computer so that when customers called, I was forced to completely change my focus and give my attention to the person I was talking to rather than to whatever I had been doing when the person called. After all, without those customers, I wouldn't have anything to do in the first place!"

Characteristics of Condition III Thinking

Condition III is called *Responding* because it is the thinking and acting we do as a reflex to a situation, without considering different perspectives, outside influences, or the full range of consequences. Unlike Conditions I and II, Condition III is characterized by our acting without the benefit of input from sources outside ourselves and without devoting time and energy to deliberation. We simply respond.

This kind of thinking allows us to move through life without a great deal of mental effort, using our experiences and our personalities to make things go smoothly. It's habitual and allows us to function without totally exhausting our brains at the end of each day.

"You don't need to write anything down for me or say anything else. I heard your argument, and I'm going to respond as I always do. The answer is No. And I don't want to discuss it further—my mind is made up."

Points to Remember About Condition III Thinking

In Condition III thinking,

- No time or energy is given to consider other viewpoints or alternatives.

- No benefit of outside input is applied to the thinking.

- Decisions are based on our individual biases and limitations.

- Knowledge of how our thinking biases lead to strengths and weaknesses is very important.

- For some people, intuitive impressions can be more accurate than deliberative conclusions.

- We defend our weaknesses by rationalizing our perspectives.

- When Condition III is inappropriate, sometimes a simple change of focus is enough to improve our responses.

Condition III—Responding	
Gain thinking energy from others?	No
Benefit of others' perspectives?	No
Time and energy to think?	Little
Effects of personal bias on decisions	High
Average portion of all thinking modules used	33-67%
Decision errors and/or regrettable actions	**Some**

We do our best thinking only a little of the time. Most of our thinking activity occurs as a response to our environment, and lack of deliberation can get us into trouble. Over time, though, most of us have developed strengths in our Condition III thinking that allow us to function smoothly. In fact, sometimes our biases and blind spots are so suited to a particular situation that it is actually counterproductive to leave Condition III thinking and switch to Conditions I or II!

On the other hand, those same biases are often inappropriate, and our blind spots often lead us astray. It's so easy and comfortable to continue using Condition III that we rationalize unsuitable behavior—we make excuses to let our familiar, domineering thinking committee members keep calling all of the shots.

This tendency to rationalize unsuitable Condition III responses might lead you to conclude that Condition III thinking is the source of most of our problems. Not so.

The final thinking condition is the one in which the *Reactor* takes over the committee at gunpoint and has his way, irrespective of the consequences. It's the condition that very often results in error and regret. Why, then, would anyone utilize this condition? We'll explore that question in the next chapter.

The Four Thinking Conditions

Deliberate Thinking		Automatic Thinking	
• Energy assigned to thinking before acting or deciding • Time taken to consider different perspectives • Gain the benefits of others' input and perspectives		• Energy assigned to acting or deciding—no energy for thinking. • Time is not taken to consider different perspectives • Subject to our own thinking biases and limitations	
Condition I	**Condition II**	**Condition III**	**Condition IV**
Relating	*Reflecting*	*Responding*	?
• Low stress	• Low stress	• Daily demands • Get things done!	

68

*Discover Your
Blind Spots:
How to Stop
Repeating
Everyday
Business
Mistakes*

Chapter 6

Condition IV—Reacting

"How could you do that? What an idiot! I can never count on you to do anything right!"

"Don't talk to me about what the other departments do! You should never have spent that kind of money on marketing! And quit talking to me about how you feel—I don't care how you feel. Just get your work done. I'd better not catch you spending money again that we haven't approved. If I do, you'll be fired on the spot!"

When your life is in peril, you do whatever you perceive is directly necessary to save it. When something important to you is threatened, you don't take time to think before acting.

The same principle applies when the hazard is to your job, your reputation, your authority, or anything else you value highly. And your actions have but one goal, irrespective of any other consequence—protect whatever is vulnerable or in jeopardy.

This is Condition IV thinking: *Reacting!*

Condition IV thinking is automatic thinking, like Condition III, but it is more immediate and more urgent. This is survival mode! No time or energy is expended in making decisions in Condition IV, even though Condition IV is often a highly energized state. Action taken as a result of a Condition IV process is swift and certain. Generally, there is no hesitation and certainly no deliberation. In some ways, "Condition IV thinking" is a misnomer. Not much active *thinking* is going on. Condition IV is an automatic-response system that follows the thinking patterns we have developed but does not involve evaluation in any real sense.

In Condition IV Reacting, all but one of the members of the thinking committee go into hiding and relinquish authority to the member that can counter the perceived threat. This committee member, which I call the *Reactor*, acts without asking permission or input of the other members.

Condition IV—Reacting—is the thinking condition in which you are more likely to make errors in judgment and do or say things you will regret later.

Forms of Condition IV Thinking

Perhaps more than with any of the other thinking conditions, Condition IV varies with the individual and situation involved. Some folks seem never to be in Condition IV—they are able to reason and devote energy to the deliberative thinking process no matter what the circumstances. Still others seem to be in Condition IV most of the time, always making mountains out of molehills for no apparent reason.

Environmental circumstances have a bearing on the likelihood that we will react or respond defensively. If you have no deadlines bearing down on you, are well rested, are healthy, and have no financial pressures, chances are far less that you will react inappropriately than if you are exhausted, in debt, hurried, or harried.

> A number of physical conditions can make a person much more likely to react. Not getting enough sleep is one such physical condition.
>
> Dr. J. Christian Gillin, M.D., professor of psychiatry at UCSD, proved this particular condition: "Brain activity is visibly altered in a number of regions following sleep deprivation" (cf. Dr. Gillin's article in *Nature*, February 2000).

A business manager may act out of Condition IV when he perceives that his professional reputation is at risk or that the financial stability of the company is in peril. He may not stop, sit down, and reflect on the situation reasonably but just lash out at whomever he deems to be threatening the things important to him.

An employee is often in Condition IV during his performance review. He may feel that the reviewer is questioning his loyalty to the company, assailing his competence, or jeopardizing his expected bonus. As he slides into Condition IV, physiological as well as psychological changes take place. His palms get sweaty. His heart rate rises. He starts to fidget. He becomes defensive and hypersensitive to criticism.

Another employee may have the opposite reaction while in a Condition IV situation. When asked to make a presentation or speak publicly, the person may react by being quiet and reserved and losing all confidence. His body may manifest all sorts of signs of stress: an upset stomach, a dry mouth, an increased heart rate, and rapid breathing. In these cases, the person's reaction is not outward but inward. This inward reaction is the result of the same kind of single-focused Condition IV Reacting that cripples or limits one's effectiveness.

Benefits of Condition IV Thinking

Condition IV thinking is always an emotion-laden response to a perception that something valuable is in danger. As such, it is unreliable and virtually impossible to regulate once it engages. However, it can be advantageous and even vital *if* the perception is accurate.

The more fundamental and basic the threat, the more likely it is that Condition IV will be beneficial. If your physical safety is at imminent risk, a Condition IV response will alleviate the danger much more effectively than Condition III. Conditions I and II would be out of the question. When the threat is real and lives or property actually *are* on the line, Condition IV is the suitable mode of response. There just isn't time for the whole committee to meet and weigh the options.

Police officers are often in Condition IV, particularly when apprehending a suspect or responding to a domestic disturbance. They know that the potential for danger is high and that they may have to act quickly and decisively. The need to protect themselves and others requires that they switch into Condition IV—any other thinking condition could cause them to get killed.

Another context in which Condition IV focus is valuable is in highly charged, physical activities, such as performing emergency surgery, flying fighter jets, or playing professional football. When you know exactly what is required of you in the moment and have had training that has prepared and tested your reactions, this emotionally fueled single focus enables you to perform in ways you could not in any of the other three thinking conditions.

Under circumstances such as these, training is a necessary component of the formula for successful Condition IV actions. Continual practice and reinforcement enables police, firefighters, pilots, emergency-response personnel, and professional athletes to develop the skills necessary for their reactions to be appropriate and constructive.

Even when Condition IV actions are appropriate, it is important to remember that Condition IV restricts a person's perspective to a single issue—the blind spots grow geometrically! In most daily contexts, this thinking limitation is inadequate for the situation and leads to greater problems.

Characteristics of Condition IV Thinking

Condition IV is *reacting* because it is automatic thinking coupled with imperative action directed toward a single goal—protecting something deemed threatened. There simply are no other considerations or perspectives.

This singleness of purpose and urgency of action is what differentiates Condition IV Reacting from the other thinking conditions. For the span of time that one is in Condition IV, every other thinking module is blind, deaf, and mute. No energy is used determining the course of action, no other perspectives or issues are factored, and all energy is expended toward performing the action.

Condition IV is efficient. It saves lives and protects vital interests when it is appropriately used. It also gets us into trouble when the perspectives of other thinking modules are needed for the state of affairs at hand.

Only one thinking module is working when we are in Condition IV. This is what gives us laser-like focus and makes us blind to other important considerations. Our attention remains constricted as long as we are in Condition IV—as long as the threat persists. Once it passes, we move back into either Condition II or Condition III thinking.

As mentioned earlier, Condition IV can be life saving, when appropriate. When inappropriate, however, it can result in wrong action that makes matters worse than the original circumstances ever could have been.

Suppose a peer offers constructive criticism and you mistake it for disparagement, right before you complete a report on department production. While in Condition IV, you decide not to include in the report the culprit's valid idea for increasing efficiency. Later, the person conveys the idea to your supervisor directly. Your omission is discovered.

The supervisor, predictably, is not pleased. Your position becomes precarious, all because of an inappropriate Condition IV response. By definition, though, Condition IV made you unable to see the likely consequences at the time. Only when you slip out of Condition IV are you able to understand the problems your Condition IV thinking created.

"I can't believe I said that!" is my Condition II conclusion about something I did when I was in Condition IV.

When reflecting in Condition II, we are able to see things that are *invisible* to us when we are reacting in Condition IV.

Typical Problematic Condition IV Responses

The following responses should clue you in that the speaker is in Condition IV and that his thinking is likely to exacerbate the situation or multiply the problems.

- "What part of NO don't you understand?"

- "I don't care how you feel—just do what we agreed to!"

- "I can't tell him to do that. He'll get mad at me."

- "I don't want to talk about it."

- "Why can't you do anything right?"

- "It wasn't my fault!"

- "No way am I going up on that stage in front of all of those people."

- "I was just too nervous to tell him."

- "I'll show that son of a *#%!@ who's the boss!"

- "Am I mad? Hell, yes, I'm mad! I wish you had never been born! I can't believe you would embarrass me that way!"

Condition IV Triggers

Jerry and Tim are production managers at a mid-sized, West Coast manufacturing firm. A deadline is looming on an order for the company's largest client. Bill, a line supervisor, knows he can't fill the order by the deadline unless he can get approval from one of the managers for overtime for the second shift of workers. The president of the company sent a memo last week that overtime was slashing into the company's profits and was to be avoided unless specifically authorized by either Jerry or Tim. Bill knows they will have to justify directly to the president any overtime Jerry or Tim approves.

Bill prepares not one but two memos requesting overtime authorization. Bill understands that Jerry feels particularly responsible for quality control and that he takes threats to product quality personally. Bill takes care to reduce the potential for a Condition IV reaction to the overtime request by addressing what he understands to be—to Jerry—an even more crucial consideration: quality.

To: Jerry
From: Bill
Re: Widget Production Deadline

Owing to implementation of your recommendations, all previous quality concerns have been met. There is no question but that this run of Widgets will be the best in the industry. Despite your repeated encouragement, however, the second shift has been unable to meet the goal for Widget production. I'm requesting authorization for three days of full-shift two-hour overtime. If I push for increased production without the overtime, I'm afraid quality will suffer. Request is also being sent to Tim.

Tim, on the other hand, is a stickler for making sure workers are not wasting time or company resources. Bill knows the overtime request is likely to generate a Condition IV reaction from Tim unless he documents that Tim's primary concern of high efficiency has been addressed.

> To: Tim
> From: Bill
> Re: Widget Production Deadline
>
> The line is being pushed as hard as I can reasonably push it. I've strictly enforced break times, and tardiness is almost nonexistent. I estimate now that at current production levels, we will miss our deadline by a week. If we can squeeze in two extra hours from the second shift for the next three days, though, we should be able to make up for lost time and meet customer expectations with a timely delivery. Thus, I'm requesting approval for that much overtime. Request is also being sent to Jerry.

An overtime request is likely to trigger a Condition IV response from a manager who will have to personally justify the expenditure. Bill, however, knows what makes each of his managers tick. He is aware of what their individual concerns are and what "pushes their buttons."

Different people assign different values to things. What is important to one is often not as important to another. One thing will trigger a Condition IV reaction in one person while the same thing will not be the slightest concern to another.

When Others Are Defensive, You Are the Attacker

When people are defensive, they are protecting something they value. Something they value is under attack and is in jeopardy! They are defending what they believe is important. Defensiveness is one of the most common Condition IV reactions.

The reason defensiveness is so common is that we don't think the same ways. One person values one thing, while another person is valuing another thing. We unknowingly step on one another's toes because we are attentive to different values. Consider this common example:

Manager: "I heard from the head of the Jones Company that the shipment was incomplete and did not arrive when promised."

Employee: "What do you mean? I did exactly what I was told to do! It was either that shipping department that messed this up or someone in the Jones Company is lying! I did exactly what the order slip said to do. I can't believe you're accusing me of this!"

In this situation, the manager values satisfying the customer because he cares about the customer's feelings, it helps his career, or it preserves his good reputation. On the other hand, the employee, who in this case is hypersensitive, values being seen as loyal and dependable. When the customer complains about the poor service, the manager may or may not go into Condition IV thinking—reacting about how the lack of customer service put his reputation in jeopardy! But it is fairly certain that a hypersensitive employee will go into a Condition IV defense of what he did because he values his dependability so highly! The manager may or may not have been attacking the employee, but the employee felt that one of his core values was under attack.

Remember: Whenever a person is being defensive in front of you, *you are the attacker!* You are putting in jeopardy something that person values highly—you are attacking and therefore you are the one who is setting up the likelihood that person will flee to Condition IV reactive thinking.

The obvious remedy to throwing another person into Condition IV reacting is for you to defend what is important to that person. In our previous example, the manager, knowing that his employee is hypersensitive about trying to do things perfectly, could have approached the discussion with one simple addition: "Bill, I need your help with something that I just learned about. I'm coming to you because I've always been able to count on your loyalty to the company and I know how important it is to you that people can count on you. I need you to help me fix this situation and to help us make sure we don't have a problem like this again with the Jones Company."

When you defend and support what is important to another person, that person will have no grounds to be defensive and won't be defensive.

Know Your Triggers

Almost everyone has triggers—things they value so strongly that they are always on the edge to react when those things are being attacked, challenged, or dismissed. When you know your triggers, you are better able to develop realistic and useful strategies and habits that reduce the likelihood that you will do something you later regret.

The danger that comes from our triggers is that they send us into Condition IV thinking without any warning. A person who has a hypersensitive Outer Self thinking module will react when he feels his reputation has been marred, even if it really is not being attacked at all.

When you don't know your triggers, you will be vulnerable to believe that you are thinking accurately and acting appropriately when you are reacting with Condition IV thinking. When we are reacting in Condition IV thinking,

80

*Discover Your
Blind Spots:
How to Stop
Repeating
Everyday
Business
Mistakes*

Common Triggers

People differ in terms of how they think and therefore have different triggers—things that send them into Condition IV thinking. Condition IV thinking is a reaction—but is not always displayed by an emotional outburst. Sometimes it is a single focus to keep quiet, to be careful to not make a mistake, or to hide one's own strong emotions so things won't get worse.

The following contexts, roles, and situations are common triggers—

- Public speaking or presentations

- Disagreeing face-to-face with another person

- Being corrected in public

- Having a person angry with you or curse at you

- Making a mistake that is pointed out by others

- Having the success of your team depend on your individual success

- Being in a group of very intelligent, beautiful, or rich people

- Being in a social situation without a clearly defined "job" to do

- Having to arrive at a solution while someone is waiting for the answer

- Having to do something you have never done before

- Having to talk about money face-to-face with another person

- Facing a deadline for a project that is critically important

- Getting ready to go out of town

Do you know which situations are triggers for you and which ones are triggers for others that are no big deal for you? As it turns out, how you act around others may actually be a trigger for other people, resulting in your being a harmful influence instead of a positive influence on them.

we have lost the judgment of all other perspectives, and our other five thinking modules are effectively blind and inactive until the presenting issue is resolved. We are very vulnerable to do something that we later regret, and we are very likely to respond in a way that creates greater problems.

Reducing Your Condition IV Visits

While it is likely that you will experience Condition IV reactive thinking at times in your life no matter how well prepared you are, you can take steps to reduce the likelihood that you will do something or say something you will later regret. When your energy reserves are high, your triggers are not as sensitive and you are less likely to have a Condition IV reaction.

The likelihood that you will react rises dramatically when your body is fatigued, when you've ignored your own physical and mental health, when you've not given to or done good things for those less fortunate than yourself, when you approach difficult meetings or tasks with little preparation, or when you have not connected with a loved one on a regular basis. Here is a simple but certainly not complete list of things that will reduce the likelihood that you will use Condition IV thinking:

- Exercise on a regular basis—especially before a difficult meeting or task.

- Talk regularly with a loved one about your feelings, frustrations, successes, and dreams.

- Do something to help a person less fortunate than you.

- Prepare yourself thoroughly and practice for meetings in which you will have to do things that are difficult for you.

- Eat foods that are good for your body (are you getting the vitamins, minerals, and enzymes you need for health?).

- Have a regular time to read and pray or meditate for your own growth as an emotional and spiritual person.

Points to Remember about Condition IV Thinking

- Condition IV thinking is automatic. It is a direct link to action, not a deliberative process—you don't have time or energy to reason.

- When in Condition IV, you don't consider other viewpoints—in fact, you can't take other perspectives into account.

- Condition IV is not the result of a decision—you are catapulted into Condition IV by a perceived threat to something important to you.

- Most people have certain environmental contexts that put them on the edge of Condition IV, such as being overly tired, having to perform in front of others, mismanagement of their finances, or having a large number of commitments to fulfill.

- Protection of whatever is threatened is the only consequence that matters to the Condition IV Reactor—no long-term or unintended results can be foreseen.

- Condition IV is the thinking condition most likely to result in needless pain and avoidable heartache for yourself or others.

- You will be best served by avoiding Condition IV, unless the threat is immediate, your job requires reactive thinking, and you have been trained how to respond.

One of the most common Condition IV contexts occurs when a person is under pressure or is facing problems that don't look like they will ever be solved. The most common of these are financial troubles, serious illnesses, and being in a horrible job.

Condition IV—Reacting	
Gain thinking energy from others?	No
Benefit of others' perspectives?	No
Time and energy to think?	None
Effects of personal bias on decisions	High
Average portion of all thinking modules used	17%
Decision errors and/or regrettable actions	**A lot!**

The Four Thinking Conditions

Deliberate Thinking		Automatic Thinking	
• Energy assigned to thinking before acting or deciding • Time taken to consider different perspectives • Gain the benefits of others' input and perspectives		• Energy assigned to acting or deciding—no energy for thinking. • Time is not taken to consider different perspectives • Subject to our own thinking biases and limitations	
Condition I	**Condition II**	**Condition III**	**Condition IV**
Relating	*Reflecting*	*Responding*	*Reacting*
• Low stress	• Low stress	• Daily demands	• High stress
Thinking modules used: 6	Thinking modules used: 4 or 5	Thinking modules used: 2, 3, or 4	Thinking modules used: 1

Now that we've examined the four thinking conditions, let's take a look at how those conditions affect our decision making, direct our interactions with others, and affect our views of ourselves—and at why our understanding of those influences is crucial to our being effective with others.

Part Three

What Affects Your
Thinking Committee

Chapter 7

Your "Reactor" Silences the Rest of Your Brain

When we are in Condition IV, the Reactor has been called to service! It is his job to get things under control. He has to oversee the defense of the value that has been attacked or put in jeopardy. He takes control of the meeting. None of the other thinking-committee members have any say in the matter. None of the other modules can add their perspectives; no one else has a vote.

When the Reactor leads the person to anger or frustration, it's easy to tell that the person is in Condition IV—Reacting. When the Reactor silences all of the other thinking modules with an outward sign of dead silence or withdrawal, the reaction is more difficult to read.

"This is not what we ordered! We need a four-color, tri-fold brochure and we need it NOW! What is wrong with you people? Do I have to do every little thing myself?!"

"No more excuses! We pay you good money to see to it that these stupid computers work. I'm due in court in half an hour, and I have to have the document that this machine just lost! You've got ten minutes to find it and put it in my hand or you're fired!"

Quietly, in his head he said, "Don't volunteer me. Don't call out my name, either. I'm not going up on that stage. Period."

_____

Reacting is not logical. People in Condition IV are not able to listen to reason and are not able to consider multiple perspectives. They don't want to discuss anything and don't care about others' views of the situation. They are single focused and, as a result, are blind to anything but their own anger, stubbornness, fear, or determination. Most of their brain is blind, literally.

Fear and Focus: The Eyes and the Brain

When we are afraid, we lose peripheral vision and are able to focus only on what is right in front of us.[1] When we are threatened, we can't see out of the corners of our eyes. Whether our reaction is fight or flight, we visually perceive only what is in front of us.

Our brains act in much the same way. When we are afraid or angry, frustrated or startled, our ability to consider other perspectives is lost. Chemical reactions in the brain connect our perceptions of the problem with the areas of the brain that produce strong emotions. This connection results in strong feelings, a sense of urgency, and singleness of focus.

_____

When people are afraid, they lose their peripheral vision and have significant blind spots. When they are threatened, angry, or frustrated, they lose their peripheral thinking and have significant blind spots.

_____

When a person is in Condition IV, he is unable to think peripherally. He cannot consider anything other than the thing that caused his reaction. Here the Reactor takes center stage and seizes control of the committee meeting—no other agenda is allowed, and no one else gets to contribute until this issue is addressed!

Focus Won't Change Until the Threat Is Removed

91

Chapter 7:
Your
"Reactor"
Silences the
Rest of Your
Brain

This process continues this way until the stimulus is addressed. Once the crisis that triggered the emotional reaction in the brain has been dealt with, then the Reactor will step aside and the other thinking modules resume their roles—the other thinking modules are engaged in whatever fashion is normal for that person.

Counting to ten helps when you are in Condition IV: The time it takes to count weakens the emotional fervor in the brain so you can start considering other things that are actually relevant to the situation.

Experience tells us that a person in Condition IV cannot consider anything other than the immediate threat. A police officer may be socially aware and compassionate. If someone is pointing a gun at the officer, though, he won't be reflecting on how unfairly that person's race or religious group has been treated throughout history. He will not be pondering the costs and pain of economic and social repression that person's ancestors had to bear. As long as he is looking down the barrel of the gun, his entire attention will be riveted on it and nothing else.

Perception of Peril to Anything of Value

The threat, however, need not be life threatening to produce a Condition IV reaction—

- A taxicab is late picking up an employee for a ride to the airport. Rush-hour traffic threatens to make him miss his flight for a business meeting that evening, and there are no other flights that day.

- A thirty-page brief due for filing this afternoon disappears into Computer Purgatory, putting the case, as well as the lawyer's professional reputation, in jeopardy.

- A manager's department posts a cost overrun two days after the senior vice president made clear that staying in budget is the company's top priority.

- A co-worker makes inappropriate and unwelcome sexual advances.

Whenever someone believes that something he values is at risk, Condition IV is likely to result. His brain goes into protection mode. The Reactor takes over and runs the thinking committee until the threat is removed. Whether the menace is real or imaginary does not matter. He will act with high energy and single focus until his perception of danger is relieved.

Believing that something of value is in jeopardy—whether the danger is real or only perceived—triggers a Condition IV reaction.

Single Focus Often Leads to Regrets

Recently I visited with a woman whose thinking biases caused her to be very black and white. The demands of her job were taxing, and when she went home in the evenings, she was drained. All of her energy resources were depleted. Time to rest and "recharge her batteries" became very important to her.

93

Chapter 7:
*Your
"Reactor"
Silences the
Rest of Your
Brain*

One evening she was feeling particularly haggard. The day had seemed to be an unending stream of people through her office, each expecting more from her than the last, until the only thing she could think about was a hot bath, solitude, and silence.

When she arrived home, her husband was excited about something that had happened at work, and he wanted them to go out to dinner. She thought that was a horrible idea.

"I don't want to go anywhere or do anything."

"But, Honey, this new project could be something really special. I want us to go celebrate a little," he said.

"I don't want to celebrate. We can celebrate another time. Leave me alone. I need some peace and quiet."

He frowned. "You don't like me very much, do you?"

At that moment, she viewed her husband as being just like the people who had been streaming through her office all day wanting something from her. His desire to go celebrate threatened her need for relaxation. In that instant, under those specific circumstances, she didn't like him very much. Her needed rest was threatened and she was out of energy, standing on the edge of Condition IV. As a result, she reacted to his question with, "That's right!"

His face fell. He stared at her for a few seconds, then turned, grabbed his coat, and walked out the door.

Immediately she realized that her need for R & R was not the only issue in the situation. She loved her husband and normally cared about his feelings. She cared about her friends and family, so it was important to her to be kind to them. She knew that her husband had always supported her in her work, and she felt a loving obligation to do likewise for him.

At the instant when she reacted, only one of her six thinking modules was engaged: the Reactor! Her tranquility, made vulnerable by a crusher day at work, was threatened by her husband's exuberance. Her Reactor took over and acted to eliminate the immediate threat, irrespective of any other consequences. And it was only after the Reactor's agenda had been taken care of that the other modules were able to contribute. As soon as her Intuition and Empathy module and her Practical module got engaged, she saw the problems with her response.

Condition IV reactions are always fraught with risk for exactly this reason: they are void of consideration of any consequences other than dealing with what is right in front of us at that instant. Other relevant and perhaps crucial factors are ignored.

Condition IV thinking has a single focus—fix what's broken, protect something valuable in jeopardy, or defend against perceived attack. It blinds us to other significant considerations. This is why, later, we usually regret Condition IV reactions. "I wish I had not said that!"

Calming the Reactor in Others—Getting Reacting People to be Reasonable

One of the fundamental differences in the thinking conditions is the amount of energy devoted to thinking and considering different perspectives. When Condition IV arises and a person is reacting, *no* energy is devoted to considering multiple perspectives. All of the energy involved in the transaction is devoted to action against the perceived danger. Thus, the key to moving people from Condition IV to a more reasonable mode—putting the Reactor back in the box, so to speak—is to ameliorate the threat. Only by removing the perception of peril can we improve the behavior.

95

Chapter 7:
Your
"Reactor"
Silences the
Rest of Your
Brain

Timing, as the saying goes, is everything. Don't bring up other matters when a person has no energy to devote to considering them. If someone is in Condition IV, deal only with the stimulus that put him there.

Lawyers are a confident lot. Much of their professional time is spent in adversarial situations, so self-assurance is an advantageous trait. They sometimes tend, however, to be overly confident. For instance, it is not uncommon for lawyers to believe that they don't need to attend computer training sessions provided by the firm's IT department.

Those same lawyers often make mistakes with their computers that can lead to their losing or corrupting important documents, which, in turn, makes it difficult for them to meet urgent deadlines. The naturally ensuing crisis usually results in Condition IV behavior—cursing, throwing the laptop computer, impugning the legitimacy of the IT director, that kind of thing.

It's not a good idea for the computer technician who is in the middle of responding to the crisis to point out that the situation might have been avoided if the attorney had attended the training classes. To the lawyer in Condition IV, those classes are worse than irrelevant. In fact, mentioning them would be perceived as another threat—to the lawyer's self-esteem—which would add to the already out-of-control Condition IV behavior!

Rather, the tech should take pains to assure the attorney that the problem will be fixed immediately—and then fix it. Later, when the deadline has been met, perhaps the lawyer will be able to consider the advisability of attending the classes so he can avoid similar problems in the future.

When you identify that someone is reacting in Condition IV, you need to see the reaction for what it is. Develop the ability to employ effective tactics to change the condition or wait until the "crisis" is over before bringing up other issues.

Ignoring Condition IV Guarantees Unwanted Results

Chances are excellent that, if you charge ahead with your own agenda when the person you are dealing with is in Condition IV, the results you obtain will be different from what you want.

One of your best employees made an off-hand comment to a reporter without making sure it was "off the record." The remark was printed out of context and could easily be interpreted as an accusation of fiscal mismanagement by the company controller—who just happens to be your boss. The controller calls you and the other employee into his office, screams for a while, and then says to you:

"Now get that lamebrain out of my office! If I see his stupid face around me any more today, I'll personally fire him."

You try to reason with him. "You're being a little irrational, boss. He thought he was off the record, and that reporter took things completely out of context."

97

*Chapter 7:
Your
"Reactor"
Silences the
Rest of Your
Brain*

"Now you're supporting him?" The controller's face reddens. "Maybe you should escort him off site and just keep going with him! I don't need this kind of insubordination around here!"

Pretty clearly, the controller simply was not able to think about the context of the remarks or to view things from the employee's perspective. Rather than trying to get the controller to act rationally under those conditions, you should have quietly taken the employee away and waited until things settled down before discussing the context of the remarks. Even better, in the interim, you and the employee might engage in some Condition I thinking about ways to counteract the news story and restore some of the controller's lost prestige.

Condition IV reactions are not always that direct or highly charged. But don't be fooled: the same single-focused, blind-to-alternatives thinking is at work.

For example, your manager is a practical thinker. He knows you have to spend money to make money. Your department has one of the highest expenditure budgets in the company, but it consistently produces revenues beyond the projections.

Other departments have not been faring as well, however. The company is in the red, and a meeting of all department managers was called for today. While your manager was gone to the meeting, a prospect you've been developing called and indicated that they are ready to close your deal, if you can commit to a production schedule that will require spending beyond your quarterly budget for raw materials.

Your manager calls late in the day. You answer the phone.

"What a killer meeting," the manager says. "The execs are really on the warpath, and they're not discriminating in terms of production. Everyone, and I mean *everyone*, took a lot of abuse for the way the company is bleeding money. I feel like I've been through a wringer."

"Sorry about that," you reply, not really listening. "But listen, while I have you on the phone, Widgets Ltd. called today, and they're about to jump. I just need to guarantee them third-quarter production. We're maxed on our purchase allocation already, but I can close this deal if you will okay a fifteen-percent excess expenditure."

"Are you out of your mind?" the manager asks. "After the beating I took today, I'm not approving any spending over budget, no matter what it's for. Don't ask again."

When a person is reacting, he has only one concern. Address that concern, and he will be able to reason with you. Ignore that concern, and he will react all the more.

Your manager was in Condition IV when he called. His position in the company was in jeopardy, albeit unjustly so, and expenditures were the key. The far better approach would have been to wait—even overnight—until some distance had come between the meeting and your request. Then, your request should have been focused on the extra revenue that would be generated by the deal rather than on the need for over-the-line spending.

Test the Waters Before Jumping In

This case is a very common example of how Condition IV reactions in others often go unnoticed. Be deliberate in developing an ability to check how people are doing before you talk with them about what is important to you. Just as effective negotiators enter their work knowing they may have to delay having their concerns addressed, try to prepare yourself for and listen for a "busy signal" before going forward with what concerns you.

99

Chapter 7:
Your
"Reactor"
Silences the
Rest of Your
Brain

Key Points to Remember About Dealing with Condition IV Reactions

- People in Condition IV—people who are reacting—are not able to consider other perspectives or consequences until the pressing concern (the threat) is addressed.

- Getting a person to move out of Condition IV requires time and necessitates that energy be devoted to thinking. In many cases, this shift out of Condition IV to I or II will best be done at another time and in another context.

- Effective communicators recognize when a person is in Condition IV and don't bring up other matters until the person is in Condition I or II contexts.

> When a person is in Condition IV—feeling that something important is or has been threatened—that person is *unable* to consider other choices or perspectives until the threat is removed.
>
> Therefore—don't try to reason with a person who has "road rage."

It's pretty clear that Condition IV presents a barrier to productive communication and effective action. Some of the same problems can exist in Condition III as with Condition IV, since they are both "automatic response" modes of thought. In the next chapter, we'll look at ways to circumvent the pull of Conditions III and IV and to use Conditions I and II to their greatest advantage in our business activities.

Notes

1. "Tunnel vision, also referred to as visual perceptual narrowing, is a process that occurs when one is visually aware only of central visual information, while simultaneously ignoring or being unaware of information located in the peripheral field of vision. During this process, high attention and detailed focus is concentrated on central processing, while awareness of peripheral information is suppressed or ignored. Tunnel vision is a response to certain types of stressors, and is closely linked to visual attention factors." (Edward C. Godnig, O.D., "Tunnel Vision: Its Causes & Treatment Strategies," http://www.oep.org/Godnig14-4.htm.)

Conditions I and II— Critical for Successful Communications

As we've seen, sometimes we act without giving much consideration to the consequences of those actions. Sometimes we devote a great deal of time to weighing the likely outcome of what we do or say. "Greatest vision" and optimum results usually flow from the two deliberate thinking conditions, Conditions I and II. We are able to move ourselves into Condition I or II thinking—when we are most likely able to see clearly—by setting aside specific time and energy for the task.

"June, could you do me a favor? I've written a speech that I have to deliver to the executive committee next Tuesday. Would you mind setting aside a half hour tomorrow to read it aloud and make whatever comments or suggestions you have on a separate piece of paper? I sure would appreciate your input."

"Boss, I'm sorry to bother you after a long day of travel. I know you're exhausted. I just want to know when would be a good time for us to discuss a new hire for the open marketing position. I'd like to revisit a couple of the candidates, even though they might be a stretch. When in the next day or two should I give you a call to discuss it?"

"What are your thoughts on the matter?"

"I know it's important—I just can't think about it right now. Give me a call tomorrow at 7:30 and we'll talk."

Pay Attention to the Busy Signal

A telephone busy signal is annoying. It's not just that the noise is unpleasant. It's that we can't have what we want, when we want it. We want to talk to the person we called *right now*. We don't want to have to call back later.

But a busy signal is actually a good thing. It lets us know that the person we are trying to communicate with doesn't have the time or energy available to devote to that task—he is occupied with something else. He may *want* to be talking to us. The busy signal tells us, though, that he isn't available to do so.

If, when we get a busy signal, we go ahead and talk over the incessant beeping, one thing is certain: the person we are trying to communicate with will not get the message.

You wouldn't talk about what is on your mind over a telephone busy signal. So then why ignore the non-phone busy signals you get every day?

The Busy Signal Is a Gas Gauge

Conditions III (Responding) and IV (Reacting) are *automatic* thinking conditions. Little or no energy is expended in thinking about the question or problem. Most of our energy is assigned to carrying out the decision or moving to another matter.

Conditions I (Relating) and II (Reflecting) are *deliberate* thinking conditions. A great deal of energy is set aside for thinking and considering different perspectives in these two conditions.

The amount of energy available for the task—how much "thinking gas" is in the tank devoted to that specific job—is one of the fundamental differences between the automatic and deliberate thinking conditions. If a person is busy, he may be using all of his available thinking gasoline on a different chore and have none available for your situation. Why is this important?

103

*Chapter 8:
Conditions I
and II—Critical
for Successful
Communications*

As we have seen in earlier chapters, someone who is in Condition III or IV can't take part in a meaningful interaction with another person. He has no thinking energy to give to what you need him to consider.

When we talk with people, we want and expect that they will give consideration to our thoughts, ideas, and point of view. Unless they have and are willing to expend enough energy to think about what we have to say, we are wasting our time. Effective dialogue simply can't take place.

A person who is busy doing something else, talking to someone else, or reacting to a crisis does not have the energy necessary to devote to your question or problem. Meaningful dialogue with him just isn't possible. Trying to communicate under those circumstances breeds frustration and misunderstanding.

Meaningful interaction and dialogue is not possible in Conditions III and IV.

The Computer—An Obvious Busy Signal

In today's business world, computers are ubiquitous. They are literally everywhere, and everyone uses them in some fashion or another. Even hard-boiled senior executives, who swore ten years ago that they would never have "one of those things" in their offices, now spend at least part of their day staring at a computer screen. And when they—or anyone else—are doing so, they are sending out a very loud busy signal.

Everyone has a friend who thinks he can carry on a conversation while his eyes are glued to a computer screen. When that friend is looking at a computer screen, he is not devoting energy to thinking about what others are saying. This is so in almost every such instance, unless what is on the screen is the *subject* of the conversation.

In the computer situation, it's fairly easy to discern that the person is busy. His eyes don't meet yours. His answers to questions are perfunctory and rapid, if they come at all. You get the feeling you're being ignored. And you are. That is the point of a busy signal—to let you know that the person you're trying to talk with is otherwise engaged and *can't* pay attention to you right at that moment.

Busy signals can be loud and clear in other circumstances, too. A person could turn and walk away in the middle of a conversation. He might abruptly change the subject, answer a question you didn't ask, or start talking to someone else. These kinds of actions are obvious clues that something other than your concerns is tapping his thinking-energy reserves.

Other busy signals are not so loud or clear. Most people don't want to be rude. They will try to make you think they are focused on what you have to say, even when they aren't. Your manager may keep glancing at his watch or may read papers on his desk when talking to you. If so, chances are that his mind is elsewhere. Looking at the time or shifting attention to something written is a subtle way of letting you know that other things are on his mind.

105

*Chapter 8:
Conditions I
and II—Critical
for Successful
Communications*

A person looking at his computer, reading papers on his desk, or sending other busy signals is probably in Condition III—on autopilot. He may not be as out of touch as when he is in Condition IV, but he is still in "auto mode" and not giving energy to consider perspectives that differ from ones he normally has. Your request or problem, all by itself, is not going to be enough to pull him out of it most of the time. You may have to speak directly to the issue, "Would another time be better for us to discuss this? I will need your undivided attention on this matter."

If you want others to consider what is important to you, then you need to lead them into Condition I or II. People don't consider different perspectives or have meaningful interactions when they are in Condition III or IV.

Toward a System—"Good Question, Bad Timing"

My wife and I have college-aged twins. When the twins were younger, they often had invitations to do things that required that a family rule be suspended. They might have wanted to go to a friend's house for dinner on a night that normally was a "family night." A special event might have been scheduled for a school night or required a curfew extension. Generally, their requests were reasonable and the things they wanted to do worthwhile.

Almost invariably, the twin with the invitation would approach her mother immediately after school. If her mother believed that the occasion was a bad idea, permission was denied and that was the end of the matter. However, if her mother thought it was a worthwhile activity, she would say, "It sounds good to me, but you'll have to get your father's permission, as well."

I'm blessed with a wonderful job. It can, however, be taxing. Typically, more than 70 percent of my time is spent talking with people about significant issues, expending a great deal of thinking energy.

During the three hours between the mother-daughter conversation and my coming home from work, the twins' anticipation would build to a fever pitch. By the time I arrived home, my energy reserves were very low. I was in either Condition III or Condition IV and not very receptive to new perspectives or alternatives. I wasn't mad or frustrated; I was just out of gas that could be assigned to thinking.

I would open the door and the twins would pounce. Since I was in an automatic thinking condition, my immediate response to their request was almost always negative: "No, tonight is family night" or "No, that would mean being out past your curfew" or "Are you kidding? Not on a school night."

My mental condition was such that I could not even take into account the positive aspects of the request—I simply responded from the platform of "the rules." It was the course of action that required the least amount of energy.

As time went by, with my wife's help, I thought about the twins and this repeating pattern of our interacting. I realized that we were blessed with very good, responsible children who, more likely than not, would not ask to bend or break the rules unless the opportunity was worthwhile. My predisposition to say "no" was more often inappropriate than appropriate. Thus, I came up with an alternative behavior. Rather than reflexively responding with "no" in these situations, I substituted "Good question—bad timing" as my automatic response.

107

*Chapter 8:
Conditions I
and II—Critical
for Successful
Communications*

This phrase represented two important facts: I acknowledged to the twins that (1) I had confidence in their judgment and (2) *when* they asked for permission to do something was a crucial factor in whether I was able to actually consider their requests. "Consider" is the operative word in genuine communication. When I had no energy to devote to the task of thinking, I was not able to *consider* their requests from their standpoints.

I Need an Answer Now!
But . . . Timing Is Everything

Certainly, it's not possible to wait until all of the conditions are perfect for optimum communication in every instance. Sometimes, the press of business dictates that we need answers to questions at times when a discussion would best be deferred. It is critical, however, to be mindful of the other person's condition if you want to have any hope of effectively conveying ideas and generating considered decisions.

So often in my business, I hear people say things like, "I can't believe he rejected the offer! It was such a great opportunity, and he didn't even think about the potential it represented for the company—he just said "No!"

Typically, my unspoken reply is "What did you expect? That's the way he acts when he is in an automatic-thinking mode. If you wanted him to think about different perspectives, you would have had to present the opportunity in a setting in which he could have interacted with you about it or at least have taken the time to ponder it. Instead, you presented it to him when he was busy, and you expected an immediate decision. You got the only response he could give you under those circumstances."

If you want to be an effective communicator, you have to develop an understanding about how much energy the person you're talking to needs to expend to fairly contemplate what you want him to consider. One gauge of this is how much time and energy you devoted to it before bringing it up to him. How often we expect others to immediately embrace what we have thought about for hours or days!

Pick the Best Time

The next time you approach someone who is busy, ask yourself which is more important to you:

1. For him to *consider* what you are talking about.

   OR

2. For you to get an immediate answer to your question.

If you want the person to consider your perspective before answering, you must take steps to get him into Condition I or II. Otherwise, you are sure to receive an automatic, and often unwanted, response.

Effective Communicator's Manifesto

1. **If I pay attention to what is important to you, then you are free to pay attention to what is important to me.**

109

*Chapter 8:
Conditions I
and II—Critical
for Successful
Communications*

If a person is in Condition IV and is reacting to something, or if he is busy with something else, he can't consider anything else until the point of focus is addressed. You simply cannot reason or effectively communicate with a person in Condition III or IV until whatever is occupying his attention—whatever put him in that condition—is addressed or set aside.

2. **I have to carefully watch for busy signals.**

In face-to-face conversations, people's busy signals are usually subtle and indirect, since they don't want to be rude or appear inattentive.

3. **To be effective, I must yield to factors of timing and the thinking condition of my listener.**

From my standpoint, there are a thousand reasons another person should stop what he is doing when I want him to and consider what is important to me. But that is not realistic. I must be sensitive to my listener and weigh the best times to bring up sensitive subjects, new ideas, or different perspectives. If I don't, chances are I will be unsuccessful and frustrated.

Practical Illustrations

- **Don't correct a speaker right after he's given his talk—**

Even if you are right and all of your thoughts are well organized and coherent, or even if he asked you for your opinion. People who have just given a presentation are usually in Condition IV—they are concerned with their image, the message, or whether they have survived the ordeal. They are unable to seriously consider new perspectives or to respect criticism, no matter how well intended. Delay your conversation until both of you can be in Condition I.

- **Don't correct your manager in front of his boss—**

Even if you are right. Even if the facts have been misrepresented, the grammar is incorrect, or the figures are inflated. If you correct him in front of his superiors, you will immediately send your manager into Condition IV. His focus will be on saving face, on your insubordination, or on something initiated by your behavior, and he will not be able to consider your information, viewpoint, or the depths of your loyalty!

- **Don't bring up a new issue and expect immediate consideration—**

Even if it is obvious to you that the matter is good for the person with whom you are talking. Energy is the key to any person's being able to consider things from different perspectives. Energy is needed to weigh new perspectives or ideas. Energy is needed to consider—be sure that you are not getting a busy signal and that the person with whom you are talking has energy to give to your concerns.

> **If you find yourself saying in your head, *"You're not listening to me!"* . . .**
>
> . . . It should be a signal *to you* that your audience is in Condition III or IV and that you either have to get the person to move to Condition II or I or wait for another time or circumstance better suited for the conversation.

Suggestions for Creating Conditions I and II

How do you go about creating the environment for effective communication? In other words, how do you move your listener from Condition III or IV to Condition I or II? Here are some things that work with different people:

- Share a meal with them. Usually, when two people take the time to sit down to eat, they are able to devote the time and energy necessary to think and discuss.

- Before you approach someone to discuss an important topic, anticipate that he may be busy, and set an alternative time in your own mind to have the conversation. That way, you will be more attuned to his busy signals. If you receive one, you will be more likely to recognize it and will be more willing to heed it.

- Put your question or idea in writing. Tell him that you would like his input on it. Ask him to set aside a few minutes to read it and jot down some notes about his ideas. People are often willing to give energy to things when they can control the time of the day when they give it attention.

- Arrange to meet somewhere other than the norm. For instance, most office settings include a conference room. Ask to meet with the person there rather than in his office. The less familiar surrounding will lessen the likelihood of distractions and will encourage him to focus on what you have to say.

- Offer to help him with whatever he is doing or with something you know he needs to get done (and then follow through with your offer). You remove whatever is engaging his interest and make him want to focus on what is important to you—as a natural quid pro quo for your help.

- Simply be sensitive to what is going on with your listener. If you focus on him for a moment rather than on your problem, you usually will be able to tell if he is in a condition to be receptive to the discussion. If you determine he is not, use your common sense—come back later, set an appointment, help him with what he's doing, or use whatever other strategy comes to mind to remove the obstacle that is preventing a communication link.

P. S. Husbands, your wife is right ...

You can't be listening—considering what she is talking about—when you are reading the paper or watching TV. *Considering* requires energy and attention to others' perspectives, and the paper and TV have taken your thinking energy. So ...

... Move to where you won't be distracted by other things when you are talking with someone—even if that person initiated the conversation and the topics or concerns that need to be discussed are his.

Part of effective communication is knowing your listener. Another part is knowing yourself. As we'll see in the next chapter, what you think of yourself often doesn't jibe with what others think.

114

*Discover Your
Blind Spots:
How to Stop
Repeating
Everyday
Business
Mistakes*

So Much for Handling Others—Let's Talk About You

An Accurate Self-View Is Critical for Managerial Effectiveness

A s I mentioned at the beginning of this book, when people ignore or misunderstand the effects of the different thinking conditions, they form ideas of themselves that bear little resemblance to what others think of them. These differences trigger frustration, impede performance, and cause people to repeat mistakes that otherwise could be avoided. The problems that come from people having inaccurate self-views are the reason so many companies do 360 reviews. Such reviews are written "score cards" as to how subordinates, peers, and supervisors view one's performance. This tool is intended to help people develop a more accurate self-view and therefore be able to be more effective in their roles and better able to build on their strengths. The following is a common situation:

Dave is a dynamic and successful salesman. He is fearless when it comes to cold calling and charming enough to make even the most resistant prospect at least listen to his spiel. As often as not, once they listen, they buy.

116

*Discover Your
Blind Spots:
How to Stop
Repeating
Everyday
Business
Mistakes*

But Dave doesn't just sell for the company. He is also a manager. While he concedes he is better at selling than at managing, he believes he is a better manager than most in the company. He also feels that he doesn't receive enough credit for his contribution as a manager and that others are jealous of his contribution.

Dave's colleagues have a different view of him. They admit he is a talented salesman but say his exceptional sales skills don't translate to equal managerial competence. They are unanimous in their observation that at times he is very disruptive and disrespectful of others, has high turnover in his team, and has more complaints arise in his department than in any of the other departments in the company.

Each year, Dave undergoes a performance review; and each year he is surprised that he is not evaluated as being one of the best managers. He has even been told that some senior managers have expressed the opinion that his productivity as a salesman doesn't justify the problems he causes as a manager. Despite these negative reviews, Dave remains blind to the fact that the problems in his department are the result of his responses and reactions and that his actions are not those of a good manager.

Self-Image Filtering Systems

Most people develop their concepts of themselves and define in their own minds who and how they are when they are reflecting, using their Condition II (Reflective) thinking. They reflect and take time to think about themselves.

In the process of self-defining, we assimilate and sort information received from all sorts of different sources. The tools we use to perform this function are what determine the outcome—they are the values and standards we use to evaluate and compare the information being offered us. When the information is consistent with our ideas about how we are, we will accept it. When it is inconsistent with what we want to be, we will either reject it as mistaken or change how we remember it. Let's call the combination of these values and how we define ourselves our "self-concept filter."

117

Chapter 9: So Much for Handling Others—Let's Talk About You: An Accurate Self-View Is Critical for Managerial Effectiveness

Your self-concept filter is actually a combination of your biology (how you were made) and your biography (how you have developed over the course of your lifetime). Therefore, it is the product of how you remember and interpret your childhood experiences and the things that have happened to you in adulthood.

Your self-concept filter is affected by the feedback you have received from others—at least the feedback that matched what you believed to be relevant to you. So if part of your self-concept filter includes the belief that your work can always be improved, then when you receive a compliment from someone, you will tend to dismiss or ignore it because it does not fit through your self-concept filter. On the other hand, if you believe you are a kind person, then someone thanking you for doing a kind deed will be part of the input you receive and remember.

I think you can see that the values and ideas you have about yourself—the kind of person you believe you are—greatly affect what you will tend to remember or forget. Your values and beliefs are a key element not only in creating your self-concept filter but also in applying or not applying the input that streams into your consciousness every day.

My View of Me vs. Your View of Me

Remember that the vast majority of our actions are responses and reactions, the result of Condition III and IV thinking. But when we use our self-concept filters and form our ideas about who we are, we are reflecting about ourselves and are therefore using our Condition II thinking. Because we typically use more of our thinking modules when we are reflecting, our perspectives and conclusions will be different in Condition II thinking than in Condition III thinking. Therefore, a disconnect often arises between how we see ourselves and how others see us.

We prefer to define ourselves using our Condition II thinking. Because I intend to be a good person or a good manager, I believe I am the person I want myself to be. I am aware that I intend to be good and I believe that those good intentions are seen and understood by others. I may recognize that in rare situations I act in ways I don't want to act, but I dismiss those as not being the real me. I see myself as a good manager and assume that others do, as well.

This is why people are on their best behavior when they are in the company of someone very important to them. This is also why managers are often so well behaved when management consultants or analysts are around but are not well behaved when such observers are not present. Those managers act out of Condition II thinking—reflecting on how to act because they want to be sure they are seen in a good light.

Another key here is that our self-concept filters tend to make us ignore or revise our actions that are inconsistent with how we define ourselves. The difference between what I believe and what I see happening has been titled "cognitive dissonance." What I see and what I believe don't fit together. When we have this kind of disagreement in our brains, we long for immediate resolution so everything will make sense again. If I believe I am an effective and supportive supervisor and I publicly berate an employee for a minor mistake, I am likely to alter my memory of what happened to satisfy the dissonance between my view of myself and my bad behavior. I will mentally rewrite the scene to achieve harmony, which may lead me to conclude that I simply gave the misguided worker some constructive criticism, or that I was calm in my explanation, or that I never called him a name, and so on.

119

Chapter 9: So Much for Handling Others—Let's Talk About You: An Accurate Self-View Is Critical for Managerial Effectiveness

---

My values, beliefs, and desires—my self-concept filters—are able to blind me from seeing my actions that are inconsistent with how I define myself.

On the other hand, the times I do act in concert with my ideas about myself will stand out in my mind. I want to be a caring, kind, and supportive boss. Thus, the occasions when I am responsive and respectful will validate my views of my effectiveness as a manager, even though I have more turnover and complaints than any other manager in the company.

In the normal course of our days, other people do not filter out those actions that are inconsistent with how we think about ourselves. They define us by including all of our actions. Our actions happen when we are in all four thinking conditions, with most of them coming from our Condition III responses. Others see us as we are revealed by all of our actions, not just the ones that make us look good and not just the ones that are consistent with our own views of ourselves. When others see that we are sometimes impatient and demanding, they will not define us as patient, understanding individuals. Others define us by everything they see us do, while we are often not aware of everything we do.

Another thing to remember in this context is that while others are assessing you based on all of your actions, they are using their own self-concept filters to do so. Because most people want to believe the best of themselves, they may have a tendency to unjustly evaluate others.

If the choice is between . . .

"I am competent, and my boss is unfair"

and

"My boss is fair, and I am incompetent"

. . . guess which one most people will opt to accept?

Toward a Clearer Understanding of Self

Since I began serving as an executive coach and professional development specialist in 1987, I have observed that those in senior management positions who have fairly accurate self-images are consistently more successful and have fewer problems than those whose self-definitions are less accurate. The progression makes sense—when people are more honest with and about themselves, their Condition II views of themselves are clearer and more accurate. When your self-concept filter allows an honest appraisal of your strengths and weaknesses when you are responding and reacting, you will be better able to modify your behavior to more closely resemble the values, beliefs, and desires you hold dear.

Furthermore, you are less likely to get yourself into circumstances that require skills and abilities that you lack, thereby setting up high-stress and high-urgency (Condition IV) situations. You are more likely going to recognize your weaknesses and accommodate them in advance of their becoming liabilities. You can plan and arrange circumstances so you can compensate for, rather than depend on, your limitations.

121

*Chapter 9:
So Much for
Handling
Others—Let's
Talk About You:
An Accurate Self-
View Is Critical
for Managerial
Effectiveness*

Managers who recognize that they aren't adept at delivering painful news to those they supervise will write down what they want to say or will enlist the help of a colleague when having to deliver such a message. Bosses who know they aren't sensitive to special personal occasions appoint someone on their team to be in charge of remembering and celebrating birthdays and anniversaries within the department. Trial attorneys who know that they have difficulty reading people will hire jury consultants to help shore up that weakness when going to trial.

Steps You Can Take

One of the most important things you can do in formulating a clearer, more accurate self-image is to listen to and reflect on the feedback you receive from others. Keep in mind that filtering doesn't occur just in the context of self-assessment. It applies in all of our interactions with others. If someone likes us, he will tend to accentuate the good we do and minimize the bad. The converse is just as true—if another person's image of us is negative, he will emphasize our failings. So while we are not to take what others say as the absolute truth, we also are able to use the input we receive from others as valuable and useful input.

- If it is common that people try to talk over you or cut your conversations short—then you may not be effectively engaging with them. They are giving you feedback that something is broken in the chain of communication because they are not showing interest in what you are saying.

• If others tend to not want to disagree with you, then it is very possible that you are so stubborn or close-minded that they have decided that it is not worth the effort.

• If people rarely offer to help you, you may appear to be unapproachable or ungrateful or to be someone who does not appreciate others' help.

One way of getting feedback is to ask for it—honestly and without strings attached. If others are willing to give it di-

A second, more objective way you can get help in developing a more accurate self-awareness is using the Hartman-Kinsel Profile. From a simple 20-minute task that you do online, a report is generated that gives you an objective model of how you think and make decisions, your thinking biases, and your own personal blind spots. While many people consider it a "personality" test, it is actually much more useful on many fronts. And better than going into the details of how it differs, the response of a lead industrial psychologist for a Fortune 50 Company recently said, "I've taken every personality and psychological inventory available to industry. The Profile is the only report I refer to over and over again. It not only helps me at work, it helps me in every facet of my life." (At the end of this book is information about how you can learn about your own blind spots and how you can get products based on the Hartman-Kinsel Profile for you or your business.)

rectly, comparing their interpretations of your actions with your ideas about what you do can be very helpful.

Now that we know what the thinking committee is, how it operates under different general conditions, and what the likely outcome of different functioning patterns is, it's time to look at some common business examples. How do these problems appear in the workplace? What simple adjustments can you make to avoid the most common problems that people make in business?

Part Four provides an examination and analysis of some of these predicaments and solutions.

123

*Chapter 9:
So Much for
Handling
Others—Let's
Talk About You:
An Accurate Self-
View Is Critical
for Managerial
Effectiveness*

124

*Discover Your
Blind Spots:
How to Stop
Repeating
Everyday
Business
Mistakes*

The
Thinking Committee
At Work

Good Hiring Practices— Interviews Hide Future Behaviors

Almost every business and professional-services firm I know ignores the differences between the condition of being in an interview and the condition of working day in and day out. Unless your interviewing practices take the TC Effect seriously, candidate interviewing will continue to be a hit-or-miss proposition. For example . . .

Your company has an opening for a mid-level manager. Human Resources solicits applications and collects résumés from all of its traditional sources. You and the HR director sit down and cull them, selecting only those résumés that reflect the education, experience, and qualifications you believe will be necessary to ensure satisfactory performance in the position.

You call in several candidates for interviews. After the first round, you narrow the field to four prospective candidates. After another round of interviews, you reduce your choices to two.

During the final interviews, you are very careful to find out which of these two obviously bright, articulate people knows more about the operations of your business. You want your decision, after all, to be based on what is best for the company and not just on your gut feeling of which person you like better. Finally, you make your choice. You wish the other finalist the best and strike a deal with the new hire. He starts to work the next Monday.

Things begin to fall apart immediately. Within a month, half of the people the new manager supervises have resigned or have lodged complaints. Production is down by ten percent, and costs are exceeding budget for the first time in a year.

What went wrong?

Unfortunately, this scenario is often the rule and not the exception. As a consultant, I hear comments like the following all the time:

"When I interviewed Jim, he gave no indication that he was so dogmatic and stubborn. When we were visiting, he was so reasonable and open—how could I possibly have predicted what a problem he would cause?"

"I had long talks with this sub-contractor before we hired him. He was so nice and took the time to explain everything he planned to do in such detail! Once he got the job, though, he was sloppy, habitually late, and completely unresponsive. He was like we had never talked at all. How could he be so different?"

"What happened? We had no idea that Susan had such an attitude! What a mistake it was to hire her—and give her a contract, no less! We've got to get rid of her, but it's going to cost big bucks to get out of this mess."

Interviews Display Deliberate Thinking—Work Requires Automatic Thinking

As was noted in the preface, industrial psychologists have proven that no statistical correlation exists between a person's job interviews and that person's future job performance. In other words, interviews as they are normally conducted are not reliable methods to get information about whether a candidate will be successful in the job. Interviews do not fulfill their intended function—helping decide among candidates and selecting good employees. You may shudder at the thought of hiring someone you haven't met ahead of time, but in most instances, interviews are no more productive than teatime.

131

*Chapter 10:
Good Hiring
Practices—
Interviews Hide
Future Behaviors*

Methods do exist, however, to increase the likelihood that meeting with a candidate actually will be helpful in determining whether he is suited for the job. When considering different candidates, keep in mind that three "matches" are important for ongoing success:

1. Is this the best candidate in terms of performing the skills needed to successfully do the tasks of the job itself? It is amazing that many applicants are never tested by interviewers to perform the basic skills and functions necessary for the position for which they are being considered.

2. Is this the best person in terms of working within our particular company, its culture, its environment, and its values? It is very common for a company to hire a competitor's superstar and have that person fail inside the totally different culture.

3. Is this the best candidate to work with the assigned manager? It is very common for an excellent administrative assistant to fail when placed under a different manager within the same organization, doing the same kinds of work.

To make interviews useful, you also need to consider the effects of the four thinking conditions and how those effects play out in the workplace, with different people, and with different jobs.

Job interviews display a variety of thinking conditions, most of them deliberate. The process of reflection (Condition II) begins before the interview. The candidate wants to make a good impression, so he devotes a good deal of thinking energy to everything from preparing his résumé to which suit and tie he wears. He may even ask other people for their feedback, relating with them about his decisions and gaining the benefits from their perspectives. During the interview itself, the candidate is usually in Condition II, reflecting on everything he says and does and being careful to be respectful and to answer questions thoughtfully.

The interviewing environment is controlled, and candidates usually have an opportunity to measure their responses. As a result, the interview may be little more than evidence of how good the potential hire is when functioning in Condition I or II, relating and reflecting.

Most interviews do contain elements of Condition III thinking, however. During most conversations, it is impossible to reflect on every answer, so the candidate will be forced to respond (Condition III) some of the time. This is particularly true if the interview involves lunch. Eating a meal tends to relax folks, making them more prone to use automatic responses to everyday situations.

Few interviews, however, put the candidate into anything like a realistic work environment. The workplace is not always planned and controlled like the typical interview setting. Working requires that we be able to function effectively using our automatic-thinking conditions (Conditions III and IV). As a matter of fact, the most common difference between effective and ineffective managers lies in how they function or don't function under stress. Almost all managers are effective in Conditions I and II; it's Conditions III and IV that separate the failures from the successes. Because most of our workplace decision-making requires automatic thinking, it is crucial that the candidate be required to use his Condition III (and possibly Condition IV) thinking in the interview, just as he will have to use Condition III thinking effectively once he is hired.

133

Chapter 10:
Good Hiring
Practices—
Interviews Hide
Future Behaviors

Good vs. Poor Employees

Condition I and Condition II thinking usually has very little relevance in differentiating between good and poor employees or managers. Most employees function well when everything is under control and they have plenty of time and energy to think clearly and deliberately. The difference between wanted employees and unwanted employees is how they perform when the pressure is on—when they have to perform in new areas or in difficult, high-stress situations.

Very good employees are capable of exercising sound judgment when responding or reacting in Condition III or IV. A crisis situation is an opportunity for a superior employee to demonstrate leadership, resourcefulness, and a stabilizing influence. Inferior employees, however, only worsen the predicament into a catastrophe because their responses and reactions exhibit bad judgment, defensiveness, or destructiveness.

As a general rule, people don't get fired for what they do when they are being careful and deliberate or for the way they respond in Condition III to the demands of the daily grind. Most people who are hired in the first place are able to carry the ordinary burdens of their jobs using their automatic, responsive thinking, even though the interview process normally doesn't test this ability. (More typically, the interview process tests for employees who meet the requirements for education, training, or experience.)

Rather, most people are discharged because they react inappropriately or destructively in high-stress, urgent circumstances. A bad Condition IV reaction often obliterates all of the good work done while relating, reflecting, or responding. It simply is a fact of business life (and of life in general) that harmful reactions carry more weight than the beneficial things done as a result of the other thinking conditions.

Competence is expected—the troublesome things get noticed. The good we do counts for little if our reactions are damaging or make a bad situation worse. Often, people are hired for their strengths and are fired for their weaknesses that neutralize those strengths.

Making Interviews More Effective

The person you're considering hiring will have to perform in all four thinking conditions while on the job. Doesn't it make sense that the interview process should include all of the conditions to give you a sense of how an applicant functions in all of them?

Since most candidates will expect the interview to be a controlled process, it will require some effort and reflection to design a process that includes Condition III and IV situations. The effort likely will be rewarded, though, in revealing the candidate best suited to the actual job.

135

Chapter 10:
Good Hiring
Practices—
Interviews Hide
Future Behaviors

Psychologists report that people have a very difficult time maintaining their deliberate thinking when they are playing a sport or a game. It doesn't have to be something that requires a lot of physical exertion—ping-pong, billiards, or throwing darts will do. It's easy to introduce stress into these situations—in fact, keeping it out would be difficult. Playing sports or games with the prospective employee will give you an indication of how he tends to behave when "all of the marbles are on the line."

Another idea is to have the candidate perform a project related to the employment. Be sure, however, not to give him all of the items he needs to complete it with ease nor to give him enough time to finish the task. While this approach may seem unfair, it is usually more realistic, since in most businesses we don't have everything we need to do our jobs and often do not have enough time. Assigning him a difficult project will let you see how the person performs under high demands and will let you see his work product, as well.

Some companies arrange for the receptionist to be a silent partner in the interview process by observing the candidate while he waits for the "real" interviewer. Occasionally, the interviewer will be late on purpose—after all, few of us work in an environment where everyone is always on time. The receptionist can comment to the effect of "Can you

136

*Discover Your
Blind Spots:
How to Stop
Repeating
Everyday
Business
Mistakes*

believe he's making you wait?" and see how the candidate responds. Many candidates will maintain their Condition II thinking and not say anything. Some, however, may reveal prejudices about people being on time and will move quickly into Condition IV, reacting to the perceived insult because they don't know that the receptionist's interaction is part of the interview.

The receptionist might also ask some of the interview questions, as if in everyday conversation. The responses the can-

---

An available tool that can help

The ZeroRisk HR hiring system (available at www.ZeroRiskHR.com) employs the Hartman-Kinsel Profile to generate a personalized interview that helps employers better consider the candidate in relation to the job, the culture, and any particular boss to whom that person will report.

It helps interviewers by directing their attention to specific biases that could be strengths or causes of weaknesses that the interviewer is able to investigate.

After one year of using the ZeroRisk HR product, a large car dealership in Texas reported the following:

"Since we began using the ZeroRisk Hiring System to help in our sales selection process, our retention has jumped from 10% to 77%. And not only do the employees stay longer, but they are more productive, catch on more quickly, and require less time in training … it has made us significantly better at hiring and retaining our sales force."

—HR Director

didate gives to a person he believes has no decision-making authority are often different from those he gives when he believes the responses count.

A variation on this method of interviewing has been used by an airline known for its unconventional methods. Candidates are told that they will have a very short time to write a zany presentation that they will have to present on stage to a group of fellow candidates. They are also told that the interviewers will be videoing during the presentations. What they are not told is that the interviewers will be reviewing how the candidates are acting when they are in the audience, not reviewing them when they are performing their presentations on stage. This way the interviewers are able to watch how fun-loving, responsive, involved, and alive the different candidates are when they do not think they are being watched. Candidates who wash out are the ones who are too focused on preparing their presentations, are not responsive to their fellow candidates, or are focused primarily on their own concerns. This way, the interviewers are able to watch the candidates in Conditions III and IV (while they still have to prepare their presentations for when it's their turn) and identify those candidates who are responsive to and engaged with others more than they are concerned about themselves.

137

Chapter 10:
Good Hiring
Practices—
Interviews Hide
Future Behaviors

The important thing is to realize that the interview must provide insight into the candidate's Condition III and IV responses and reactions, not just into how effectively they function in Condition I and II contexts. Chances are that the selection process—through résumés or specific prerequisites for application—will provide candidates who will be able to function adequately in Conditions I and II, and even in most Condition III circumstances. To make a decision about which person is the right one for the job or for your company—the one who will be a real asset rather than a potential detriment—you need to know more about him than traditional interview techniques reveal.

You need to apply your own Condition I and Condition II thinking to design the interview process and set up situations that will let the candidate's true colors show!

Everyday in business in situations other than prospective employee interviews, we often see that what people say doesn't match what they later do. In the next chapter, we'll explore why this is so. We'll see how a correct understanding of the TC Effect will enable us to reduce the number of these occasions and lessen their impact.

Chapter 11

In Meetings, People See—When Working, They Don't

When it comes to the frequency of ignoring the TC Effect, meetings top the chart. For most people, a large part of every day is spent in discussions with other people, coming to agreement on how to handle a given problem or situation. Those meetings usually end with specific assignments being made—someone in the meeting undertakes to act in a particular way, as agreed by all of the participants of the meeting (even if there are only two participants). Sometimes, the person does follow through, doing what he agreed to do. But often, he does not.

Executive: "Now, Bill, we've discussed all the possible ramifications. I want to be sure we're clear on this. We simply can't afford to have this thing mishandled. It will be best for you to approach this person fairly. Be gentle and understanding. Don't be accusatory just because this involves an allegation of sexual harassment. Don't you think it best that you speak cordially and calmly and behave in a conciliatory manner?"

Manager: "Yes, I agree. I understand what's at stake. I'll be patient and understanding."

You can see what is going to happen. Once Bill leaves the meeting with the executive and begins his meeting with the person who filed the complaint, his perspective—how he thinks about and interprets the offender's behaviors—will change because the condition is different! He will see and think about things differently. Because of his thinking biases, he will become confrontational and accusatory, the problem will escalate, and what might have been solved quickly and inexpensively becomes a costly calamity. Why?

To understand this, we need to examine the thinking conditions involved.

In with One Brain—Out with Another

The Bill who was meeting with the executive is a different Bill from the one who met with the employee. He is a different person in each set of circumstances—at least to the extent that he is defined by how much of his brain he is using and by the manner in which he is using his brain.

In most cases, meetings with others are conducted in Condition I—we are relating to others. Remember our earlier discussion of the six thinking modules? When we are relating in Condition I, we are often using all six of those modules (Intuition and Empathy, Practical, Structured, Inner Self, Outer Self, and Self-Concept). We benefit from the energy and perspectives provided by the people with whom we are relating. Using that energy and being stretched and encouraged by them, we arrive at solutions we could not develop on our own.

People relating in Condition I see things more clearly than they ordinarily do when thinking on their own. They also come to believe they can act in ways that they normally cannot. Relating to others in Condition I provides moral support and courage to tackle problems that ordinarily would seem too complex or overwhelming.

Once the meeting is over, however, and Condition I ends, people move into whatever thinking condition is dictated by the circumstances they next encounter. They start using their brains another way and, to that extent, literally become a different person. In the business context, people most often move from relating in Condition I to responding in Condition III. While this doesn't have to be a problem, in many instances or for some people it can be the source of continual troubles.

141

*Chapter 11:
In Meetings,
People See—
When Working,
They Don't*

Different Context
= Different State of Mind
= Different Person

In a meeting, we are **relating** with others in **Condition I**. When we leave the meeting, we are in a different state of mind. That state of mind can be—

Condition II—we are deliberate, **reflecting** on what was said; or

Condition III—we are **responding** automatically to our surroundings; or

Condition IV—we are **reacting**, focusing on only one aspect of the situation.

All three are different from the state of mind we were in during the meeting. That difference will often lead to our looking at the situation in a totally different way than we did when relating during the meeting.

Recall that, as we saw in Chapter 1, each of us has natural thinking biases that affect how we evaluate everything, particularly when reflecting and responding. When we are relating to others in Condition I, the effect of those biases is minimized because of the energy and insight we gain from the others in the meeting. Once we leave the relating context, however, those biases can override conclusions and agreements made during the meeting. When we are on our own, reflecting in Condition II, responding in Condition III, or reacting in Condition IV, we often see things differently and reach different conclusions about the best way to approach a given situation or dilemma.

Don't you see people act differently depending on who enters the room? The TC Effect explains why people act differently when their boss or a person they recognize as an authority enters the room.

A Different Twist on the Same Problem

What if Bill's conversation with the executive had gone more like this:

Executive: "What? Another sexual harassment allegation! All right, Bill, let's see if you can do at least one thing right. You deal with this situation and do it gently and fairly. Do not fly off the handle the way you normally do and go pointing fingers. We absolutely cannot afford to have you screw this thing up. Do you agree that you will speak cordially and calmly and behave in a conciliatory manner?"

Manager: "Yes, Sir. I absolutely agree. I will handle this thing with kid gloves. You can depend on me."

Once again, Bill leaves the meeting with the executive and begins the meeting with the person who filed the complaint. He quickly becomes confrontational and accusatory, exactly the opposite of what he agreed to do. Why?

This time the meeting with the executive was not a Condition I interaction in which the participants were relating with one another toward a common goal. Rather, it was an encounter in which both of those involved were reacting in Condition IV to perceived threats. The executive saw a threat to the company, and Bill recognized a risk to his job. Bill quite simply would have said whatever it took to remove that threat.

143

Chapter 11:
In Meetings,
People See—
When Working,
They Don't

Just as with the situation in which the parties are relating, once the meeting is over, the type of thinking changes. It could go from Condition IV to Condition I, II, or III, depending on the circumstances, or even to a different Condition IV, as Bill's evidently did. But remember—in Condition IV, the focus is only on resolving the threat or the value that is in jeopardy.

In Bill's case, the apprehension he felt when speaking to the executive was a fear *of the executive*—the executive was the source of the threat. When he confronted the complaining employee, his focus changed to the employee and the sexual-harassment complaint that caused him to fear *for his job* or for his status within the company.

If you go from a high-stress or confrontational meeting where you are reacting with Condition IV thinking and move into circumstances that require you to respond or reflect, you are required to develop a broader, more reasonable perspective. Whatever you agreed to do while reacting in the high-stress meeting may appear to be too harsh or unreasonable when you consider those choices using your Condition II or III thinking.

A common example of this is a manager whose boss demands that he be confrontational with an employee on his team. The boss rails at the manager about how the employee is disruptive and costing the company money and resources. The manager agrees to deal with the matter directly and immediately. He will tell the employee to shape up or he's fired.

The manager, however, is a person who likes to gain and retain the approval of others, including his employees. After meeting with his boss and the immediate threat of his boss's disapproval has passed, the manager focuses on maintaining the employee's approval . He leaves his boss's office and begins to think differently. He knows that the employee has stresses at home and other demands outside of work. He considers that the employee might not be able to stand much pressure at the office.

So, rather than taking a stance against the employee, the manager comes alongside him, encouraging and gently cautioning him. The employee, meanwhile, never gets a sense of how much trouble he is facing. While we don't know if the manager's failure to do what he agreed to do is a service or a disservice to the employee, there is no doubt that it is far from what he agreed to do when meeting with his angry boss.

Most of the time, the way people think when they agree to do something during a meeting is different from the way they think when it comes time to act out the agreement. This is not to say that people will usually not do what they agree to do. In fact, most of the time, people will follow through and perform as they agree to. It's just to point out that almost all people think differently when interacting and relating to others than when thinking alone and that it is therefore naïve to assume that everyone will do on his own what he agrees to do in front of others.

145

Chapter 11:
In Meetings,
People See—
When Working,
They Don't

Common Solutions to the Problem

When you're meeting with someone and he agrees to do something after the meeting, picture in your mind that the "meeting person" is not the same person who will be doing the task. The conditions we find ourselves in determine how we think. Don't fall into the trap of supposing that people are always the same, irrespective of the circumstances they find themselves in.

Take these factors seriously:

- How the person's thinking differs when he is on his own than when he is in a meeting.

- How the condition of the meeting differs from the conditions in which he will have to fulfill his agreement.

- How the person typically acts when asked to do something on his own.

The following three methods are regularly used to increase the likelihood that a person will do what he agrees to do:

1. **Accompaniment**—"I'm thinking that it would be a lot easier for you if I were with you when you address this matter. What do you think?"

2. **Written Contract**—"Let's put our agreement in writing so it's clear what we each agreed to do and so we'll know exactly when each of us has completed his work."

3. **Follow Up**—"After you're done, I'll give you a call so we can discuss how it went."

While these methods won't guarantee that people will act as they agree to act, they reinforce the agreement, irrespective of how it conflicts with their later mode of thinking. The most effective managers know their direct reports so well that they don't assign them tasks to do on their own that they are not likely able to do, even when the direct report asks to do that task. Effective managers often know how their reports act when using their automatic thinking better than the reports know themselves.

Just as everyone has different thinking biases, everyone in a management position has a different preferred style of managing people. In the next chapter, we will examine the three common types of styles and how the different thinking conditions apply to these management styles.

Chapter 12

No One Is a Natural Manager

Most people operate at work using their Condition III, automatic responsive thinking. While this is crucial to be able to continue to function (otherwise we'd be too exhausted from thinking to ever be able to do anything), there are times when managers need to schedule time and energy for Condition I and Condition II thinking. But most managers ignore the negative effects of the TC Effect on themselves while going through each day and dismiss the positive effects of rest and recreation that Condition I and II thinking requires.

"Let's face it—people can't be trusted. For most of them, it's just a job. They don't care. So they make mistakes, they forget, they're sloppy. If I weren't there telling them exactly what to do, showing them how, we'd never reach the production levels we need. I was hired to make sure things get done right the first time, on time and under budget. To make that happen, I've got to be there, all the time. If there were a hundred others like me, I'd be able to do it all myself. As it is, I make sure they do it my way."

"I can't stand the idea of not being involved with my team, making things happen, being part of the energy and dynamics. It's not right to hire people and just leave them floundering. I need to provide encouragement, make the work fun, and lead by example. Besides, we do a heck of a better job when we're all in there together."

"These folks know what they're doing. I get out of their way and let them do it. That's why I hired them. If there is trouble, they know to come to me. Otherwise, I stay out of their way and let them do their jobs."

There are three basic styles of management—directing, coaching, and delegating. Directors tell people what to do, how to do it, and when to do it, leaving as little to chance as possible. Coaches lead their teams by becoming involved with them, interacting with the members, giving encouragement, and providing direction and feedback. Delegators identify and communicate the goal, make sure the team has the equipment to reach the goal, and then get out of the way, turning their attention to other matters.

Three Management Styles

Directors   Tell people what to do, when to do it, and how to do it

Coaches   Provide encouragement, direction and redirection, and support

Delegators   Equip and leave them alone

Condition III Determines Our Preference

Each of us has a style of management that we prefer over the other two. Our thinking biases and blind spots that are apparent in our Condition III thinking determine those preferences. As a result, we are inclined to use our preferred style, even when it is not the appropriate style for the occasion or with that direct report.

Remember the thinking biases that direct your thinking committee that we identified in Chapter 1 and discussed in the previous chapter? Those same biases are what we use in our Condition III responsive thinking and thus control which management method we rely on and which methods we really prefer not to employ.

For instance, if your thinking biases dictate that you don't use much of the Intuition and Empathy thinking module, then you will have a difficult time trusting other people. This bias causes you to be naturally and automatically suspicious of others' intentions. You will be more comfortable as a director and will prefer to tell people what to do and how to do things, even when it would be more productive to let them work on their own or when they are very trustworthy people.

If, however, you are naturally attentive to Intuition and Empathy thinking but don't personally think about yourself with your Inner Self module or your Outer Self module, you will tend to put people on a pedestal in comparison to yourself. This orientation will cause you to prefer to delegate, making it difficult for you to direct or tell other people what to do.

(Now, be careful at this point in the discussion that you don't start arguing that it is better to value others more highly than you value yourself. When your natural thinking biases cause you to reach certain conclusions, you, like everyone else, will come up with life philosophies that support your thinking biases. It may be a sound moral tenet to give others more benefit of the doubt or consider their concerns more than you consider your own—but unless this self-surrendering is done freely and willfully, then there is no giving actually taking place. You are not sacrificing something that you value but are actually choosing what makes you the most comfortable by operating in the way that is consistent with your natural ways of thinking.)

Each of us has a preferred management style that is the by-product of our natural thinking biases. But I also have a bias about high speeds and would prefer to drive most freeway off-ramps at 135 miles per hour! It is important to keep in mind that you are the one who is doing the thinking, and if you are processing your thoughts with only certain parts of your brain, you are the one who is choosing to do so. I will drive off the road if I ignore what physicists tell me about taking an exit at 135 mph, and you will destroy or maim your team by *directing* your reports when they and the situation warrant your *delegating* to them. Ignoring what axiologists are telling you about changing your management style according to the needs of the people and the situation is like ignoring physicists' counsel about driving—you will go over the cliff.

All Three Are Necessary

Often, a particular management style is associated with a particular industry. Directors are common in movie making, building construction, and road repair (three bosses hovering over the one guy with a shovel, telling him what to do). In sports, car sales, and restaurant kitchens (as with a chef and a sous-chef), coaching is more common and suitable. Teachers at colleges, administrative assistants in executive offices, and good legal assistants in law firms, however, usually respond best to delegation.

Despite the preferred style of the industry, every manager or supervisor will be required to use all three techniques.

Context sometimes requires that a different approach be taken. Reliable and normally independent employees may need to be coached or directed through novel or high-stress situations or because of legal requirements.

Different employees functioning in the same capacity may require different management styles, as well. You might want all of your employees to be internally motivated, resourceful, and reliable, but reality paints a different picture. It's a mistake to delegate to someone who is apathetic about the task. By the same token, even the most enthusiastic worker will sometimes become confused or discouraged and will require the encouragement of a coach.

Managers tend to accept positions most appropriate to their preferred styles. To be effective, however, all managers need to be able to recognize and adjust when the situation or the person requires a shift from one method to another.

Deliberate Thinking Is Required

The ability to adapt management styles demands that a manager use his deliberate thinking. Automatic thinking is what is natural for us. This is why I state that no one is a natural manager. All people prefer to use their favorite technique, no matter what the circumstances require. Some people are better than others at shifting from one management style to another. No one, though, has thinking biases that fit all three management styles equally—so no one is naturally suited to manage all three ways.

Deliberate thinking requires time and energy. An effective manager can't be so busy that he goes from one encounter to another, one task to another, with no opportunity to stop and consider. He must be able to contemplate what the tasks are that his employees are being asked to perform, how the employees' circumstances may have changed, and what those employees need from him. Effective managers realize that they may have to set aside their automatic management style and apply a different one that is better for the situation. And they must set aside the time and energy to determine which style best fits the situation.

Effective managers set aside time and energy to think about and think through the needs of each of their direct reports.

Effective management means that a natural delegator will stay involved and direct his workers when the context requires strict oversight. It means that a person who loves to coach will understand when an employee's confidence needs a boost and when the employee should be turned loose to complete a project by himself. And it means that a person inclined to control every detail will step aside and encourage those who report to him to learn by trial and error when they are at that point in their development.

You may or may not be a manager at this time. But the principles of this chapter apply to everyone. We all do better when we pay attention to how the dynamics of situations and of others' abilities and attitudes change. I encourage you to practice responding appropriately to changing situations and to the people with whom you are interacting. Abandon those ideals that drive you to believe you should stick with the methods you started with, because those ideals were forged in a mind that did not understand the effects of the thinking conditions.

Another situation that is common to most manager-employee relationships is fraught with danger because managers ig-

A Significant Success in 1999

Ben Crenshaw, coach of the 1999 US Ryder Cup team, knew that the team was in trouble. It was the last day of the tournament. For the USA team to have any chance of winning, Justin Leonard needed to at least tie his match. He had not won any matches in the preceding three days. After seven holes, Justin was down by four strokes and clearly discouraged.

Justin is a very talented professional golfer. Under ordinary circumstances, delegation would be appropriate—get out of his way and let him play. But Ben realized that sometimes even top professionals need support and coaching. Ben asked Davis Love III, Justin's close friend, to talk to and encourage him when he came off the green.

Justin played so well after his conversation with Davis that he won his round with a forty-five-foot putt on the seventeenth hole, ensuring the greatest come-from-behind victory in Ryder Cup history.

While Crenshaw knew that Justin was such a great player that he normally could be delegated a task on the golf course, he adjusted his management style to fit the particulars of this situation. Davis Love III said it best: "We won because of Ben Crenshaw. He fired us up, made us believe we could do it."

nore the TC Effect and how Condition IV skews thinking. In the next chapter, we'll examine why what should be a productive, mutually beneficial activity often turns to disaster. And we'll talk about ways to prevent that from happening. We'll take a look at the performance review.

*Discover Your
Blind Spots:
How to Stop
Repeating
Everyday
Business
Mistakes*

Chapter 13

Coaching Through Reviews

"Oh, good! My last three reviews are all really good employees. This first one will take about five minutes—there's just one small area he needs to focus on. The other two are doing just fine, so I think I can skip them altogether."

The idea that performance reviews for the best employees require the least amounts of time and effort is a commonly held view among managers. But this is a recipe for lost opportunities. This mindset is a result of not understanding how the thinking conditions apply to the performance review process. Confusion about reviews and the value reviews can provide often results in comments like these:

"I knew Allan's review was going to be hard to do. I kept putting it off. Finally, he bugged me so much about it that I scheduled it for last Friday at 3. What a mistake! Not only did he argue with me about every point I tried to make, but we were here until eight o'clock that night! As far as I'm concerned, this whole process is a counterproductive waste of time."

"What am I doing wrong? Whenever I review my good employees' performance at year-end, they go away mad or disappointed and frustrated. One of my best people even told the assistant manager that, after his review, he was afraid he was going to be fired! That's not the way these things are supposed to work."

Performance Reviews Are Condition IV for Most

Annual performance reviews are no party. Managers often hate giving them, and employees often hate receiving them.

Assessing employees' performance takes time and attention. Managers usually feel that reviews take them away from their real work—those things that reflect directly on their job performance and reputation in the company. They are of the opinion that good employees don't need the process and the marginal or poor employees get little benefit from it. They just get defensive and angry. Constructive criticism falls on deaf ears, or—worse—it generates ill will.

Employees, on the other hand, are sometimes apathetic but usually more apprehensive about their reviews. They are nervous, like a group of high school students waiting for a teacher to hand back graded exams. They are worried that their bonuses won't adequately cover the money they've already spent or that the bonuses won't be distributed fairly. They are anxious that they won't receive adequate credit for all the good they did during the year. Clearly, for these employees, performance reviews are a Condition IV event.

The Anticipation of Criticism Induces Stress

Managers regularly describe reviews of their best employees something like this:

"Jim came into the review like he had been plugged into the wall all day. He was jumpy and breathing fast, and his palm was damp when we shook hands.

"I was very careful to go through all of his accomplishments and note all of the positive aspects of his performance throughout the year. He seemed to relax somewhat. When I turned to the two or three points I thought showed a need for improvement, though, you would have thought I had killed his favorite dog. He got such a pained look on his face, I was a little afraid he might cry. It seemed like he forgot all of the praise I had just given him."

For many managers, reviews of good employees can be as difficult as or more difficult than those of poor workers because of the pain the reviews seem to cause for the conscientious employees. Most managers don't want to cause discomfort in those who report to them, particularly when the managers really are happy with the employees' achievements. This brings up another point . . .

Reviews Are Stressful for Managers, Too

Talking face-to-face with another person is easy when we know that the subject of the conversation is of interest to or honors the other person. Discussing the other's weaknesses or mistakes, however, is a completely different matter.

Most of us don't have a genuine mean streak. We don't like to cause pain or discomfort for other people. Conversations that are likely to strain relationships and cause disagreement or defensiveness are things we avoid. Performance reviews are by definition just such conversations.

It's understandable, then, that most managers approach reviews with some degree of apprehension. That anxiety sets the manager up to go into Condition IV very quickly.

Time and Energy Are Essential

Performance reviews don't have to be counterproductive or a waste of time. They can be an occasion for honest appraisal, reflection, and renewal. Like students beginning a new school year, performance reviews can give employees the opportunity to honor the good they have done and leave the errors and disappointments of the past in the past. Reviews provide an opportunity for managers to give honest feedback about expectations, as well as to supply support and encouragement when needed.

For your reviews to be positive events, however, you must devote the necessary time and energy to them in terms of both preparation and implementation. Here are some suggestions for making performance reviews mutually beneficial times:

- **Make a Record**—Throughout the year, keep a notebook in which you evaluate each employee's work—similar to a teacher's grade book. This not only makes preparation for the review easier from a logistical standpoint but also allows you to be precise in your comments and isn't vulnerable to fallible memory.

- **Prepare and Write It Down**—Make sure you set aside enough time to use your reflective Condition II thinking when preparing for the review. Write down what you intend to cover, at least in outline form.

- **Talk It Out**—Have a trusted colleague go over the most difficult reviews with you a few days before you're scheduled to give them. This allows you to use relating Condition I thinking in the process, giving you the benefit of a fresh perspective and additional energy.

- **Get the Negatives Off the Table**—Most conscientious employees want to do a perfect job. When they are listening to a review of their accomplishments, most are waiting for the "Yes, but . . . ," which is about the things they've done wrong. They hold themselves to excessively high standards and therefore dread the inevitable problems they have to fix or errors they've made throughout the year. This dread causes them to focus on what they are going to hear and miss the good that is being presented. They are in Condition IV thinking because something they hold valuable is going to be challenged.

  It is often best to cover what they did wrong first. Get it off the table. Discuss it, interact about it and then close that subject. When the review is done this way, the employee is free to move from Condition IV reacting (which is how these kinds of employees have to think when being reprimanded) to Condition I relating about his strengths and contributions and about how good and effective his manager believes him to be.

- **Forget the Grease**—Devote more time and energy to reviews of your better performers than you do to reviews of the poorer employees, who are always squeaking. To many, this is counterintuitive. In my years of coaching executives and professionals, though, I've found that one of the most valuable things I can do is get them to spend the most time and energy with those people and things that contribute most to success. Typically, 10 percent of the people do 90 percent of the work. Those 10 percent deserve your best time and your best thinking—not the 90 percent who are just squeaky wheels clamoring for attention.

160

*Discover Your
Blind Spots:
How to Stop
Repeating
Everyday
Business
Mistakes*

- **Schedule Strategically**—Be cautious and strategic in scheduling reviews. Remember that most of them will be Condition IV events. Don't set them at the end of a busy week or when you know you will be rushed to get to the next appointment. Earlier in the day is better than later because you don't want either party to be worn out. Be proactive and make the schedule an ally of the process rather than an enemy. Anticipate a time when you and the employee will have the energy to weather the stress of the review. Don't go into a difficult situation when both of you are frazzled, tired, or just wanting the day to end.

Assume that, for a particular employee—let's call him Mark—a couple of years of reviews go well and Mark functions brilliantly. It's time to reward him with a promotion. Seems like the normal thing to do, right? Good for him and good for the company, don't you think?

Not necessarily. In the next chapter, we'll see why promotions without careful consideration of the TC Effect often do not accomplish what is intended.

Ill-Informed Promotions Can Kill a Career: Oversights When Promoting Employees

One of the most expensive results of overlooking the TC Effect comes when people are inappropriately promoted to new positions. Venture capitalists are quick to bemoan the poor track records of presidents they place in their recently acquired companies. The venture capitalists not only ignore how the TC Effect causes them to prefer people who think like they do (which my research shows is often an inadequate thinking structure for running a business) but also ignore how the TC Effect mandates that the new president not be left alone in the early stages of his new role.

But venture capitalists are not alone. They are accompanied by executive committees of law firms that promote the highest-producing lawyers to leadership positions within their sections. They are accompanied by school administrators who foolishly promote the best teachers to administrative positions. And they are joined by the thousands of companies that take their best sales representatives and promote them to management positions. But for a change of perspective, consider the following true story:

162

*Discover Your
Blind Spots:
How to Stop
Repeating
Everyday
Business
Mistakes*

Mark was the best sales manager the company ever had. He knew production figures for every field sales representative on his team off the top of his head at any time— every day of the week. It seemed that some sort of weird ESP connected him to the reps in the field—he was on the phone arranging for materials and special marketing aids even before the sales reps made the requisitions.

He went to bat for his people at all the right times, and they knew it. He built such a team feeling that his reps would cover for each other without having to be asked twice. He developed a commission-sharing system so effective that there had not been a complaint of anyone stealing leads in nearly five years. Upper management figured it was time to move Mark into the assistant vice president of operations slot.

As it turned out, upper management was wrong.

About six months after Mark was promoted, the VP of operations, Mark's new boss, walked into the company president's office and shut the door. This is what he said:

"We're in a fix and I'm not sure what to do. Mark is flailing like a beached whale and it's killing the business. We're the ones who insisted that he take the promotion, even when he expressed doubts about being able to handle it.

"Dave is doing nicely as sales manager, although not as well as Mark did. Mark certainly doesn't deserve to be fired—it's not his fault he's in a position he can't handle. But we have to do something. His delays and ineptitude are going to bleed us to death."

So the human resources director found some management courses that Mark could take to help him adjust to his new duties. They cost a lot of money that wasn't budgeted, but they helped. Mark began to perform adequately, and the company started running in the black again.

163

Chapter 14:
Ill-Informed
Promotions Can
Kill a Career—
Oversights
When Promoting
Employees

Dave continued to function satisfactorily as sales manager, although production figures flattened somewhat. One sales rep quit and went to work for a competitor, citing the "cut-throat competitive atmosphere" that developed as soon as Mark was moved from overseeing the sales force.

Mark never was happy in Operations. About eighteen months into the job, he resigned and went to work as the director of sales for the same competitor that now employed the sales rep. For the first time in history, the competitor now threatens to overtake the company in market share.

What went wrong? Could the company have prevented this fiasco?

Maybe. Sound analysis of the TC Effect could have given upper management the information necessary to predict Mark's inability to handle the new job. What they did with that information, of course, was up to them.

Why We Promote Employees

Although there may be a thousand reasons people receive promotions, the reasons generally fall into one of two categories. The first reason is that the promotion gives the person's new boss some much-needed help and relief, and the company expects to reap benefits from the greater leverage of the promoted person's skills and abilities. The second reason people are promoted is that employees have grown so much that they need more challenges or more responsibility to keep their interest and performance at a peak.

Although mistakes can occur whatever the reason for an advancement, the first category (a promotion for the sake of the company) causes the most problems.

In almost every case, employees are promoted out of jobs in which they are doing well. They know what they're doing and are doing it better than most of their peers. As we saw back in Chapter 4, when an employee is doing a good job, chances are that his Condition III thinking strengths match the skills required for that position. Seeing this performance, management gets the idea that the employee is dependable and is capable of handling more responsibility.

Businesses leverage the ability of employees. What I mean by this is that the impact of a manager's decisions is usually more significant than that of a non-manager's decisions. When a manager is successful, it means a far greater return for the company than when a non-manager is successful. A higher position requires enhanced judgment and heightened responsibility because more is riding on what the person does—the risks and potential benefits to the company are much greater.

Thus, it makes sense that before you promote a person, he should demonstrate that he has the wherewithal to perform in the position to which he is moving, not just in the position *from* which he is moving.

He Never Did It Before

You've heard the expression "Necessity is the mother of invention." In promoting employees, "Necessity is the mother of impatience, frustration, and neglect." When managers are overworked, they become impatient in wanting to get someone to help them.

165

*Chapter 14:
Ill-Informed
Promotions Can
Kill a Career—
Oversights
When Promoting
Employees*

What managers often overlook is that whenever a person is promoted to a new position, *he has never done that job before.*

In every instance, the person promoted is in alien territory. He has new responsibilities, unfamiliar political relationships, and a different reporting structure. Even when a person assumes a position in one company that he previously held in another company, the people he must deal with, the company culture, and the position of the company in the marketplace are all new and different. For him, the job is a new job.

Whenever a person is promoted, remember: *He has never done that job before!*

Remember Mark? We saw that Mark's Condition III responsive thinking strengths made him a great sales manager. Not every good sales representative can be a great sales manager. A good rep must be able to read strangers, think on his feet, enjoy a challenge, and have a desire to win. He has to be able to initiate and meet specific individual tasks on a regular basis.

An effective sales manager, on the other hand, has to be able to coordinate the efforts of a small, like-directed group. He needs to have a talent for managing the competitive attitudes of the individuals and building them into a force that benefits the company. Some sensitivity for company politics is helpful, and superior organizational skills are valuable.

When Mark was promoted to assistant VP of operations, he brought his abilities to motivate others, to learn new tasks quickly, and to prioritize effectively. But he also had to do things that were stressful for him. He had to become effective at planning strategically, making presentations to the board, and implementing and enforcing policies to large groups of people. These new roles were very stressful and sent Mark into Condition IV thinking, which made his new role one that exhausted him on a regular basis.

The Transplant Effect

Gardeners know that how a transplanted tree is treated will have an enormous impact on whether it will thrive or wither in its new location. On occasion, trees do take root and grow with no special attention. Sometimes, too, people will take to new employment positions and do well even though they were left to themselves and given no special support or oversight.

But the opposite is true too frequently. A tree is more likely to flourish if tended, nurtured, and fertilized. When managers work closely with promoted employees, coach them, and help them negotiate the landscape of their new environment, they adapt and excel far more often.

This is where venture capitalists often make their greatest mistake. Being masters of finance and numbers, they do thorough due diligence on capital and equity and make sure that provision is made for those concerns and for possible risks they might face in the future. But they throw their presidents into the new roles without support, nurture, or adequate help. They argue that a person paid that much and with that much experience should be able to succeed on his own. But the TC Effect directs us to coach people through their transitions into new positions, not throw them in with no support.

167

Chapter 14:
Ill-Informed
Promotions Can
Kill a Career—
Oversights
When Promoting
Employees

A client of mine promoted a very successful and capable employee into a management position and then left him completely alone. He received no training, no guidance from his manager, and no orientation in company politics. The reason given was that his manager was very busy. Besides, so the story went, he was promoted to make his manager's life easier, not to place further supervisory burdens on his new boss.

One of the employee's former peers, who wanted the same job, had a close relationship with the president's secretary. The sabotage was easy and successful. The former peer and secretary worked quickly and subtly to undo this new manager in the eyes of the senior management. The promoted manager was neither politically adept nor connected—so senior management had no reason to give him the benefit of the doubt. The manager was terminated within three months of his promotion. Had his boss taken the time to tend, fertilize, and prune, things might have been very different. Everyone might have seen that the new manager was actually doing a pretty good job and that the accusations of his former peer and the president's secretary were totally unfounded.

What Others Have Learned

Three primary lessons have emerged from the experience of others in promoting employees:

168

Discover Your
Blind Spots:
How to Stop
Repeating
Everyday
Business
Mistakes

1. Promoting a good employee into a position in which he fails is more expensive than waiting and filling the position more carefully.

2. A person is more than twice as likely to fail if promoted before he has consistently demonstrated the skills necessary for the new position than if he outgrows his position by exhibiting the skills needed in the new job before being promoted into it.

3. Managers cannot realistically expect a promoted person to relieve them of extra work for a few months. The manager must assume a coaching role for a period of time before he can reap the benefits of being able to delegate to the promoted employee.

Points to Consider Before Promoting Someone

- Every promotion puts the person into a role he has never filled before.

  Who is going to mentor, support, and oversee the person in the position until he is able to function in the new role?

- The skills needed for success in a new position are different from the skills needed to rise to that position.

  Has this person consistently demonstrated the abilities and desires necessary for success in the new role? The

It's Different Being Here Than Getting Here

A client was having trouble with an executive promoted to senior management some six months earlier. He was aggressive and self-promoting and didn't share with his colleagues. I was asked to work with him to get him to function more in line with the collegial team orientation of the other executives.

After meeting with him and discussing his history, I saw that the qualities that made him successful and brought him to be promoted by senior management were precisely the ones causing friction now. I ended our conversation with this reminder:

The behaviors and skills required to get into the ranks of the senior executives here are totally different from the behaviors and skills required to work effectively within those ranks.

169

*Chapter 14:
Ill-Informed
Promotions Can
Kill a Career—
Oversights
When Promoting
Employees*

higher up in an organization, the more people skills are required.

- Everyone needs someone to give him constructive correction and feedback.

    Who is going to tell this person he's messing up before it's too late?

- Everyone needs an advocate to go to bat for him when others are attacking his work.

    Who is going to watch this person's back by explaining his actions to senior management when they have only part of the story?

170

*Discover Your
Blind Spots:
How to Stop
Repeating
Everyday
Business
Mistakes*

As we saw back in the Introduction, the condition you are in and the conditions you are under affect the way you think, affect your ability to perform, and, thus, affect the outcome of virtually any situation. It is no different with people promoted into new jobs—they are strangers walking an unfamiliar road. The more you can do to make sure they have a map—and a good pair of shoes—the better off everyone will be.

Afterword

So Now What?

Each of us has natural biases, strengths, and blind spots. We use our brains in different ways—which results in our having different personalities. In addition, our brains work differently depending on the conditions we are in and the circumstances we are under. Our thinking committees comprise various members, and those members vary in their involvement, depending on the situation and what must be done.

We use the most thinking modules and expend the most energy toward thinking in the deliberative process in Condition I—Relating. We devote the least energy to thinking and use the least number of modules in Condition IV—Reacting. Correspondingly, the error rate is highest in Condition IV and lowest in Condition I.

Since most of our daily activity is a result of our Condition III responsive thinking and because no rational, deliberate activity is possible when we are reacting in Condition IV, these are the conditions that bear the most study, if we are to arrive at a true understanding of our potential—for good and ill.

Suggestions Based on the TC Effect for Management Improvement

Simply being aware of and paying attention to these thinking conditions and the factors affecting them, though, can accomplish one very important thing: it will allow you to adjust your approaches and expectations accordingly.

- Each day, sit (without paying attention to any of the hundreds of things that are always pressing upon you) and spend five deliberate minutes thinking about whom you work with, your family members, and your friends. Ask yourself the following questions:

  1. What do I have that I can give today that will make that person's life better (such as encouragement, information, feedback, support, a listening ear, and oversight)?

  2. How does that person need me to interact today?

  3. What am I inclined to ignore that I really should pay attention to?

- In meetings, keep in mind that the people who are agreeing to do something will often have a different mind and a different perspective once they are out of the meeting. Be sure to use one of the recommended bridges or some other bridge that spans the gap between what the person agreed to in a Condition I meeting and what the person does when on his own in Condition III thinking.

- When interviewing a job candidate, leave most of the talking behind and get the candidate doing something so he is using his Condition III responsive thinking and so you can see him functioning when under pressure.

- Remember that people are not islands. The condition they are *in* and the conditions they are *under* make all of the difference in what parts of them you are going to see and get. How you interact and don't interact with people is going to make a huge difference in their outcomes.

Always be asking yourself, "What can I do or not do that will increase the likelihood of this person succeeding?"

I, II, III Is Your Formula for Real Growth—

Apply the I-II-III formula for real professional growth:

Step 1. **Condition I (Relating)**—*Get input* and sound counsel from others about what is best for you to do and how you can best think about or view a particular matter.

Step 2. **Condition II (Reflecting)**—*Think about and prepare* how you are going to implement these new thoughts into actions and choices. Be deliberate in doing things in the new ways. Continue to do these new behaviors and note how you're getting better results.

Step 3. **Condition III (Responding)**—As you continue to deliberately practice the new behaviors, you will be able to *start using the new behaviors automatically*—from reasoning to deliberate practice to automatic and consistent desired behavior and outcomes.

Doing these things will ensure that you—

- Have fewer disappointments.

- Have more frequent effective conversations with others.

- Experience less resistance from others.

- Reach more of your goals.

- Reduce the negative effects of your own blind spots.

- Stop repeating everyday business mistakes!

174

*Discover Your
Blind Spots:
How to Stop
Repeating
Everyday
Business
Mistakes*

Special Offers for *Blind Spots* Readers

Free to *Blind Spots* readers . . .

Go to www.Clear**Direction**.com and take a simple quiz to discover whether you have blind spots—and what they could be!

For more help . . .

Many of our readers ask how they can learn about their own blind spots or how they can get Clear Direction products for their companies.

Clear Direction Inc. publishes the world's very first (and only) Internet-delivered book based on each individual's responses to a set of tasks that takes just 20 minutes to complete. The resulting **Profile Report** is really an individualized book put together with specific information about how *you* think. No one else's **Report** will be just like yours.

Your **Clear Direction Profile Report** provides you with two key descriptions:

1. How you think in **Condition III** when you are *responding* and going through your normal day, and

2. How you think in **Condition IV**—what you focus on and what you ignore when you are under stress and are *reacting*.

The **Profile Report** is your opportunity to discover your own blind spots and thinking strengths.

For more information . . .

To learn more about Clear Direction Inc. products for your business, contact—

sales@Clear**Direction**.com